D0416806

CANCELLED

FINDING GOBI

FINDING GOBI

The true story of a little dog and an incredible journey

DION LEONARD

WITH CRAIG BORLASE

HarperCollins*Publishers*

This is a work of nonfiction. The events and experiences detailed herein are all true and have been faithfully rendered as remembered by the author, to the best of his ability, or as they were told to the author by people who were present. Others have read the manuscript and confirmed its rendering of events. However, in certain instances names of individuals have been changed.

HarperCollins*Publishers*
1 London Bridge Street
London SE1 9GF

www.harpercollins.co.uk

First published in the US by W Publishing Group, an imprint of Thomas Nelson, 2017
This UK edition published by HarperCollins*Publishers* 2017

1 3 5 7 9 10 8 6 4 2

All photographs used with permission. Photographs from the 2013 and 2014 Kalahari Augrabies Extreme Marathon are courtesy of KAEM; photographer Hermien Webb.

A catalogue record of this book is
available from the British Library

ISBN 978-0-00-822795-1

Printed and bound in Great Britain by Clays Ltd, St Ives plc

Find out more about HarperCollins and the environment at
www.harpercollins.co.uk/green

For my wife, Lucja.
Without your endless support, dedication, and love, this never would have been possible.

PROLOGUE

THE CAMERA CREW FINISHED UP LAST NIGHT. Someone from the publisher arrives tomorrow. I can still feel the jet lag and other side effects of forty-one hours of travel in my body. So Lucja and I have already decided to make this, our first run of the year, an easy one. Besides, it's not just the two of us we need to think about. There's Gobi to consider.

We take it easy as we pass the pub, drop down beside Holyrood Palace, and see the clear blue sky give way to the grassy mountain that dominates Edinburgh's skyline. Arthur's Seat. I've run up there more times than I can remember, and I know it can be brutal. The wind can be so strong in your face that it pushes you back. The hail can bite into your skin like knives. On days like those, I crave the 120-degree heat of the desert.

But today there's no wind or hail. There's nothing brutal about the air as we climb, as if the mountain wants to show itself off in all its cloudless glory.

As soon as we hit the grass, Gobi is transformed. This dog that's small enough for me to carry under one arm is turned into a raging lion as she pulls forward up the slope.

"Wow!" says Lucja. "Look at her energy!"

Before I can say anything, Gobi turns around, tongue lolling out, eyes bright, ears forward, chest puffed. It's as if she understands exactly what Lucja's said.

"You haven't seen anything yet," I say, pushing the pace up a bit in an attempt to loosen the strain on the leash. "She was just like this back in the mountains."

We push farther up, closer to the summit. I'm thinking how, even though I named her after a desert, I first saw Gobi on the cold, rugged slopes of the Tian Shan. She's a true climber, and with every step we take, she comes more and more alive. Soon her tail is wagging so fast it blurs, her whole body bouncing and pulsing with pure joy. When she looks back again, I swear she's grinning. *Come on!* she says. *Let's go!*

At the top, I soak in all the familiar sights. The whole of Edinburgh is spread out beneath us, and beyond it is the Forth Bridge, the hills of Lomond, and the West Highland Way, every one of whose ninety-six miles I have run. I can see North Berwick, too, a full marathon distance away. I love the run along the beach, even on the tough days when the wind is trying to batter me down and every mile feels like a battle all its own.

It's been more than four months since I've been here. While it's all familiar, there's something different about it as well.

Gobi.

She decides it's time to descend and drags me down the hill. Not down the path, but straight down. I leap over tufts of grass and rocks the size of suitcases, Lucja keeping pace beside me. Gobi navigates them all with skill. Lucja and I look at each other and laugh, enjoying the moment we have longed for, to be a family and finally able to run together.

Running isn't usually this fun. In fact, for me, running is never fun. Rewarding and satisfying, maybe, but not laugh-out-loud fun. Not like it is now.

Gobi wants to keep running, so we let her lead. She takes us wherever she wants to go, sometimes back up the mountain, sometimes down. There's no training plan and no pre-mapped route. There are no worries either. No concerns. It's a carefree moment, and for that and so much more, I'm grateful.

After the last six months, I feel like I need it.

I've faced things I never thought I'd face, all because of this little blur of brown fur that's pulling my arm out of its socket. I've faced fear like I've never known before. I've felt despair as well, the sort that turns the air around you stale and lifeless. I've faced death.

But that's not the whole story. There's so much more.

The truth is that this little dog has changed me in ways I think I'm only just beginning to understand. Maybe I'll never fully understand it all.

Yet I do know this: finding Gobi was one of the hardest things I've ever done in my life.

But being found by her—that was one of the best things.

PART 1

1

I STEPPED THROUGH THE AIRPORT DOORS AND out into China. I paused and let the chaos take a good hard whack at my senses. A thousand revving engines in the car park ahead did battle with a thousand voices around me as people shouted at their phones.

The signs were written in both Chinese script and what looked to me like Arabic. I couldn't read either language, so I joined the crush of bodies that I guessed were waiting for a taxi. I stood a foot taller than most people, but as far as they were concerned, I was invisible.

I was in Urumqi, a sprawling city in Xinjiang Province, way up in the top left corner of China. No city in the world is as far from an ocean as Urumqi, and as we'd flown in from Beijing, I watched the terrain shift from razor-sharp snow-capped mountains to vast stretches of empty desert. Somewhere down there a team of race organizers had plotted a 155-mile route that took in those freezing peaks, the incessant wind, and that desolate, lifeless scrubland known as the Gobi Desert. I was going to run across it, knocking out a little less than a marathon a day for four days, then almost two marathons on the fifth day, and an hour-long sprint for the final six-mile stage that would bring the race to a close.

These races are called "multi-stage ultras", and it's hard to think of a more brutal test of mental and physical toughness. People like me pay thousands of pounds for the privilege of putting ourselves through pure agony, shedding up to 10 per cent of our body weight in the process, but it's worth it. We get to run in some of the remotest and most picturesque parts of the world, and we have the safety net of a dedicated support crew and highly trained medical crew on our side. Sometimes these challenges can be excruciating, but they're also life changing, and reaching the finish line is one of life's most rewarding experiences.

Sometimes things don't go so well. Like the last time I tried to run six marathons in a week. I ended up in the middle of the pack, in agony. At the time it felt terminal, as if I'd never compete again. But I recovered just enough for one last shot. If I could run well in the Gobi race, maybe I'd yet have some more running in me. After all, in the three years since I'd taken up running seriously, I'd found out how good it felt to be on the podium. The thought of never competing again made me feel queasy inside.

If things went wrong, as they had for another competitor in the same race a few years back, I could end up dead.

According to the Internet, the drive from the airport to the hotel was supposed to take twenty or thirty minutes. But the closer we got to the hour mark, the more agitated the driver became. He had started out grouchy when he realized I was an English-speaking tourist and quoted me a price three times as much as I was expecting. It had got only worse from there.

By the time we pulled up outside a redbrick building, he was waving his arms and trying to shove me out of the cab. I looked out the window, then back at the low-resolution image I'd shown him before we started the journey. It was kind of similar if you squinted a bit, but it was obvious that he hadn't brought me to a hotel.

"I think you need some glasses, mate!" I said, trying to keep it light and get him to see the funny side. It didn't work.

Begrudgingly, he picked up his phone and yelled at someone on the other end. When we finally made it to my destination twenty minutes later, he was livid, shaking his fists and burning rubber as he sped away.

Not that I'd been bothered. As much as ultra-running batters your body, it also assaults your mind. You learn pretty quickly how to block out distractions and mildly annoying things like lost toenails or bleeding nipples. The stress coming from an enraged taxi driver was nothing I couldn't ignore.

The next day was a different story.

I had to travel a few hundred miles out of the city by bullet train to get to the race headquarters in a large town called Hami. Right from the moment I arrived at the station in Urumqi, I knew I was in for a journey that would test my patience.

I'd never seen such security at a train station. There were military vehicles everywhere, temporary metal roadblocks funnelling pedestrians and traffic past armed guards. I'd been told to allow myself two hours to get on the train, but as I stared at the great tide of people ahead of me, I wondered whether it was going to be enough. If the previous day's taxi ride had taught me anything, it's that if I missed my train, I wasn't sure I could overcome the language barrier and re-book another ticket. And if I didn't get to the race meeting point that day, who knew if I would even make the start?

Panic wasn't going to help me get anywhere. I took control of my breathing, told myself to get a grip, and shuffled my way through the first security check. By the time I cleared it and worked out where I needed to go to collect my ticket, I discovered I was in the wrong queue. I joined the right one, and by then I was way down on my time. *If this was a race*, I thought, *I'd be at the back.* I never ran at the back.

Once I had my ticket, I had less than forty minutes to clear another security check, have my passport stared at in forensic detail by an over-eager policeman, force my way to the front of a line of fifty people waiting to check in, and stand, open-mouthed, panting and staring frantically at signs and display boards I couldn't read, wondering where the heck I had to go to find the right platform.

Thankfully, I wasn't entirely invisible, and a Chinese guy who'd studied in England tapped me on the shoulder.

"You need some help?" he said.

I could have hugged him.

I just had time to sit down at the departure point when everyone around me turned and watched as the train crew swept past us. It was like a scene out of a 1950s airport, the drivers with their immaculate uniforms, white gloves, and air of complete control, the stewardesses looking poised and perfect.

I followed them onto the train and sank, exhausted, into my seat. Almost thirty-six hours had slipped by since I left home in Edinburgh, and I tried to empty my mind and body of the tension that had built up so far. I looked out the window for something to interest me, but for hours on end the train just sliced through a bland-looking landscape that wasn't cultivated enough to be farmland and wasn't vacant enough to be desert. It was just land, and it went on for hundreds and hundreds of miles.

Exhausted and stressed. This was *not* how I wanted to feel this close to the biggest race I'd faced so far in my short running career.

I'd taken part in more prestigious events, such as the world-famous Marathon des Sables in Morocco, universally agreed to be the toughest footrace on earth. Twice I'd lined up alongside the thirteen hundred other runners and raced across the Sahara Desert as the temperature topped 125 degrees in the day and sank to 40 at night. I'd even finished a respectable thirty-second the second time I ran it. But fifteen months had passed since then, and a lot had changed.

I had started taking note of the changes during another 155-mile race across the Kalahari Desert in South Africa. I'd pushed myself hard—too hard—to finish second overall, my "first-ever podium finish" in a multi-stage. I'd not kept myself hydrated enough, and, as a result, my urine was the color of Coke. Back home my doctor said I'd caused my kidneys to shrink due to the lack of liquid, and all that running had left them bruised and resulted in blood in my urine.

A few months later I'd started having heart palpitations during another race. I could feel my heart beating wildly, and I got hit by a double blow of queasiness and dizziness.

Both those problems flared up again almost as soon as I started the Marathon des Sables. Of course, I ignored the pain and forced myself through it, all the way to a top-fifty finish. Trouble was, I'd pushed myself so hard that as soon as I got home, my left hamstring went into violent and agonizing spasms every time I tried to walk, let alone run.

For the first few months I rested; then for the next few I was in and out of physiotherapists' consultation rooms, all the time hearing the same-old same-old: I just needed to try whatever new combination of strength and conditioning exercises they were suggesting. I tried them all. Nothing helped me to run again.

It took the best part of a year to find a physiotherapist and a coach who both had running expertise and knew what was going on to discover the truth: part of my problem was that I wasn't running correctly. I'm tall—well over six feet—and while my long, steady, loping stride felt easy and natural, I wasn't firing up all the muscles I should have been using, so I had sharp, painful spasms in my legs every time I ran.

The race in China was my first chance in a tough competition to try out my new, faster, shorter stride. In many ways I was feeling great. I had been able to run for hours on end at home without pain, and I'd followed my usual pre-race diet better than I ever had before. For the previous three months, I'd avoided all alcohol and junk food, eating not much more than chicken and vegetables. I'd even cut out coffee, hoping that would put an end to the heart palpitations.

If it all paid off, and I ran as well as I thought I could do in China, I'd tackle the prestigious race that the organizers were putting on later in the year—across the Atacama salt plains in Chile. If I won there, I'd be in the perfect shape to get back to the Marathon des Sables the following year and make a real name for myself.

I was the first passenger off when we pulled into Hami and at the head of the pack as we surged towards the exit. *This is more like it*, I thought.

The guard manning the security checkpoint put a quick end to my joy.

"What you do here?"

I could see a long line of taxis outside the door, all waiting beside a vacant pavement for my fellow passengers to lay claim to them. I tried to explain about the race and say that I wanted to go and get a cab, but I knew it was no use. He looked quizzically back and forth between me and my passport, then motioned me to follow him into a trailer that doubled as an office.

It took half an hour to explain what all the packets of energy gels and dried foods were for, and even then I wasn't convinced he believed me. Mostly I think he let me go because he was bored.

By the time I got out and approached the pavement, the crowds had all gone. And so had the taxis.

Great.

I stood alone and waited. I was fatigued and wanting this ridiculous journey to be over.

Thirty minutes later a taxi pulled up. I'd made sure to print off the address of my hotel in Chinese script before I'd left Urumqi, and as I showed it to the driver, I was pleased to see that she seemed to recognize it. I climbed in the back, squashed my knees up against the metal grille, and closed my eyes as we pulled out.

We'd only got a few hundred feet when the car stopped. My driver was taking on another passenger. *Just go with the flow, Dion.* I didn't see any point in complaining. At least, I didn't until she turned to me, pointed to the door, and made it perfectly clear that the other passenger was a far better customer, and I was no longer welcome in the cab.

I walked back, spent another twenty minutes getting through

the inevitable security checks, and lined up once more, alone, at the deserted taxi stand.

Another taxi came, eventually. The driver was happy and polite and knew exactly where to go. In fact, he was so confident that when he pulled up in front of a large, grey building ten minutes later, I didn't think to check that I was at the right hotel. I just handed over my money, pulled my bag out after me, and listened to him drive away.

It was only when I walked into the entrance that I realized I was in the wrong place entirely. It was not a hotel but an office block. An office block in which nobody spoke any English.

For forty minutes I tried to communicate with the office workers, they tried to communicate with me, and the phone calls to I-didn't-know-who failed to get us any closer. It was only when I saw a taxi drive slowly past the front of the building that I grabbed my bag, ran out, and begged the driver to take me where I needed to go.

Thirty minutes later, as I stood and stared at the empty bed in the budget hotel the race organizers had booked, I said out loud my solemn vow.

"I am never, ever coming back to China."

It wasn't the frustration of not being able to communicate properly or even the muscle aches and serious fatigue that were bothering me. All day I'd fought hard against the urge to worry, but as one thing went wrong after another, I ended up getting nervous. It wasn't logical, and it didn't make sense. I'd reminded myself again and again that I had allowed plenty of time to get from Beijing to the race start, and I figured that even if I'd missed my train, I could have found a way to put things right. And I knew, deep down, that any aches I'd picked up from the previous couple of days would soon shake themselves out once I started running.

Even so, by the time I arrived at the hotel near the race headquarters, I was more anxious than I'd ever been before any race I'd ever run. The source of my nerves wasn't the journey, and it wasn't the knowledge of the physical challenges that lay ahead of me. It was something far, far deeper than that.

It was the worry that this might be my last race ever and the fear that maybe I was never going to win a race—winning had been the only thing that motivated me to run competitively in the first place.

Tuesday, 3 January, 1984. The day after my ninth birthday. That was when I first understood how quickly life can change. The day had been a great one, soaked in beautiful Australian summer sunshine. In the morning I'd ridden my bike over some jumps I'd put together while Mum and Dad read the papers and my three-year-old sister played out in the yard near Nan's downstairs flat at the far end of the house. I'd finally managed to perfect my somersault on the trampoline, and after lunch Dad and I went out with our cricket bats and a few old balls. He was just recovering from a chest infection, and it was the first time in ages that he'd joined me for a bit of sport outside. He taught me how to hold the bat in just the right way to hit a ball so hard and high that it sailed way out over the scrubby grass and beyond the far boundary of our property.

When I finally came inside in the late afternoon, I found the house to be full of the smells of Mum's cooking. She steamed her chocolate pudding for hours and made Bolognese so rich that I would hold my head over the pot and inhale the aroma for as long as I could before the heat got to be too much.

It was a perfect day.

Like any nine-year-old, I denied I was tired when it came time to go to bed, but soon enough I was drifting off to sleep, vaguely aware of Mum leaving for her Tuesday night aerobics class while Dad watched cricket on TV with the sound turned down low.

"Dion!"

I didn't want to wake up. It was dark and my head was still half-stuck in its curious dream world.

"Dion!" I heard Dad's voice again. There was no other noise in the house, no TV, and no sound of Mum anywhere.

I didn't know why he'd be calling me like this, and I let myself drift back to sleep.

I couldn't tell you how much longer Dad went on calling my name, but at some point I knew I had to get up and go and see what he wanted.

He was lying on his bed, under a sheet. He didn't look at me when I came in, and I didn't want to go too far into the room. His breathing sounded all wrong, as if he was having to use all the strength he possessed to drag even the smallest lungful of air in. Something told me he was really sick.

"Go and get your grandmother straightaway, Dion."

I ran downstairs and knocked on Nan's front door.

"Nan, you've got to come," I said. "Dad needs you. Something's wrong."

She came right out, and I followed her back upstairs. I remember thinking that because she used to be a nurse, Dad would be okay. Whenever my little sister, Christie, or I was hurt, Nan would always make us laugh as she tended to our wounds, telling us stories from when she worked in a war repatriation hospital as a head nurse in charge of the others. She was a tough woman, a fighter who I believed held within her hands the power to make any illness or pain disappear.

As soon as she saw Dad, she left to call an ambulance. I stayed with him while she made the call, but as soon as she came back, she told me to leave the room.

Christie was asleep in the next room. I stood and watched her, listening to my dad's breathing grow worse and Nan talk in a voice I'd never heard her use. "Garry," she said, a little louder than normal. "The ambulance is coming. You're having an asthma attack. Keep calm, Garry. Stay with me."

Christie woke up from the noise and started crying. "Dad doesn't feel well, Christie," I said, trying to sound strong like Nan. "But people are coming to help."

I raced across the hallway to open the door as soon as I heard the ambulance pull up outside. I watched as the paramedics carried a stretcher and breathing apparatus up the set of stairs. And I looked on in silence as Mum rushed into the house a few minutes later. I listened to the sound of Mum's sobbing coming from the bedroom, not understanding what it meant. When they wheeled Dad out a while later, I didn't want to look at him. He was still struggling to breathe, and his head was shaking. I could hear the noise of one of the wheels under the stretcher as it squeaked along.

I followed everyone outside, where the streetlights and headlights and blinking hazard lights all made the night look out of time. As the medics were loading Dad into the back of the ambulance, he told Mum he loved her. I stood by Nan's side, the grass cold against my bare feet. "Things will be okay," said Nan. I didn't know who she was speaking to.

Christie, Nan, and I stayed back while Mum went off with Dad in the ambulance. I don't know how long we were alone, or even what we did. But I remember that it was around midnight when the front door finally opened. Mum came in with a doctor beside her. Neither of them had to say anything at all. Nan and I both knew what had happened. Soon Mum, Nan, and I were crying. Not long after, the phone started ringing. Nan answered, her voice low, the calls never lasting more than a few minutes. When the doorbell rang and the first neighbours arrived and hugged Mum tight, I disappeared to my room.

On the day of the funeral, I watched as Dad's coffin was wheeled toward the hearse. I broke free from Mum's hand on my shoulder and ran out to stop it. I draped as much of myself as I could around the timber box, but it was no use. My arms couldn't reach all the way around. When my sobbing got so hard that it hurt my chest, someone peeled me away.

2

SOON AFTER DAD'S DEATH, MUM MOVED DOWNstairs, where Nan took care of her and Christie and me. It was as if Mum became a child again, and in doing so she couldn't be a mum to us anymore.

I may have been just a nine-year-old kid, but any fool could have spotted the signs. The day I walked in on her in her bedroom, tears barely dry on her cheeks, confirmed the fact that she wasn't coping.

That was a few weeks after Dad's death. It took a few months for me to find out that her troubles were not just caused by grief. She and I were in the kitchen one evening. She was cleaning—a new obsession that had started recently—and I was sitting at the table reading.

"Dion," she said, "Garry wasn't your dad."

I don't remember crying or running off to hide. I don't remember shouting or screaming or asking my mum to explain further. I have no memory of what I said next. I have no recall of how I felt. A blank void exists where so many memories should be. I can only imagine how painful that news must have been for me to wipe all trace of it from my mind.

But what I know for sure is that the wound that had been inflicted on me by my dad's—Garry's—death became so deep that it changed everything about me.

Even today my mum will cry when she and I talk about Garry's death. She'll say it took only a twenty-minute ambulance ride for everything in our lives to change. She's right, but she's also wrong: it might have taken minutes for life to be thrown into chaos, but it took only four words for my grieving heart to be ripped completely apart.

I held tight to my secret. Within a year or two of finding out the truth about myself, I was ashamed of my past: not only was I the kid without a dad at home, but I was the only one I knew who also had a single parent. The regular stream of visitors that poured in after the funeral had long since stopped, and our dwindling finances forced Mum to go out and find work. Whenever she was at home, she spent hours repeatedly cleaning the house and listening to Lionel Richie songs played loudly on the stereo in the pristine dining room.

In my mind, it seemed like all my friends came from perfect families, and because they all went to church, I'd take myself on Sundays as well. I wanted to feel as though I belonged, and I also liked the fact that I could help myself to a handful of small cakes after the service. I didn't mind the sermons so much—sometimes they even made me feel better about myself. But the way people responded to me, as I hovered near the tea table at the end of the service, made it clear to me that they saw me differently from everyone else. I could hear them whispering behind my back. As soon as I turned around, the awkward silence and fake smiles would come out.

Mum started getting phone calls as well. I'd try to creep out into the hallway and watch as she stood, her face turned to the wall, shoulders hunched. Her words were clipped and the calls short, and sometimes when they were over, she'd turn around and see me watching and tell me about the latest gossip people were spreading about us in the town.

Soon enough I encountered the ostracism myself. When I went to a friend's house to visit one Saturday afternoon, I could see his bike on the grass out front, so I knew he was in. His mum, however, said he couldn't come out to play.

"You can't see Dan," she said, pulling the screen door closed between us.

"Why not, Mrs. Carruthers?"

"You're a bad influence, Dion. We don't want you coming around."

I walked away devastated. I didn't drink, swear, act up at school, or get into trouble with the police. Okay, so I was a little greedy with the small cakes at church, but other than that I was always polite and tried to be kind.

She could only have been referring to one thing.

I didn't have a name for it at the time, but I quickly developed a strong dislike for being made to feel I was being excluded. By the time I was fourteen, I was well aware of precisely where I belonged in life: on the outside.

I sat, as I always did, alone and away from everyone else as the race staff welcomed the runners and started the safety briefing. The race was organized by a group I'd not run with before, but I'd been in enough of these meetings to know what was coming.

The biggest danger for anyone running a multi-stage ultra in desert heat is when heat exhaustion—your standard case of dehydration, cramps, dizziness, and a racing pulse—tips over into heatstroke. That's when more drastic symptoms arrive, including confusion, disorientation, and seizures. You won't know it's happening; you won't pick up the signs yourself. That's when you end up curling up in a ditch or making wrong decisions at precisely the time when you need to be getting out of the heat, replacing salts and liquid, and drastically reducing your core temperature. If you don't, you can slip into a coma and end up dead.

The race organizers said that anyone they suspected of being on the edge of heat exhaustion would be pulled from the race immediately. What they didn't say was that six years previously, one of their competitors in the same race had died from heatstroke.

The microphone was passed to an American woman. I recognized her as the founder of the race. "This year we've got some great runners competing," she said, "including the one and only Tommy Chen." There was a round of applause from the hundred runners in the room, who all shifted focus to a young Taiwanese guy who had his own personal film crew standing beside him, capturing the moment. We then listened to a whole load of stuff about how Tommy was going for the win, how he already had some great results behind him.

When I was back home, I had researched the runners I thought were the main contenders, so I knew Tommy was one of the best around. I knew he was a genuine multi-stage superstar and would be tough to beat.

Before I'd left Scotland, I'd read an e-mail from the organizers listing the top-ten runners they expected to do well. I wasn't mentioned at all, despite having beaten a few of them in the past.

A bit of me was still annoyed about it but not because my ego was bruised. There was no reason why they would have expected me to do well. Having not raced since a 132-miler in Cambodia eight months before, I felt I had become a forgotten nobody, and I didn't blame them for passing me over.

I was annoyed with myself. I'd started running only three years earlier but already had enjoyed a few podium results. Coming to the sport so late, I knew I had only a tiny window in which to prove myself, and taking eight months off to recover had felt like a waste of precious time.

Before the briefing we had a kit check to make sure we each had the mandatory equipment required for the race. Even though we carry all the food, bedding, and clothes we will need for the entire six-stage, seven-day race, the aim is to keep our bag weights to a minimum. For me, that means no change of clothes, no sleeping mat, and no books or smartphone to keep me entertained at the end of the race. All I bring is a sleeping bag, a single set of clothes, and the absolute minimum amount of food I can get away with. I bank on 2,000 calories a day, even though I know I'll burn closer to 5,000. I return home looking like death, but the lighter bag is worth it.

Later that day we were boarded onto buses and taken to the site where the race would begin, a couple of hours outside of Hami. I made small talk with a guy next to me, but mainly I kept quiet and tried to block out the noise of the three guys who had come from Macau behind me who were laughing and talking loudly the whole way. I turned around and half-smiled at them a few times, hoping that they'd pick up on my subtle hint for them to shut up. They just grinned back and carried on with their party. By the time we stopped, I was pretty fed up and hoping to get off and find some peace and quiet to start mentally preparing for the race ahead.

The locals put on a beautiful exhibition of regional dancing and horse riding, including a game that looked like polo but was being played with a dead sheep. I snuck off to find the tent I'd be staying in to claim my spot. On most multi-stage ultras, runners get assigned tent mates to camp with throughout the race. You never know who you're going to get, but you can at least make sure you don't get stuck with a terrible sleeping spot.

I stood in the old army surplus tent and wondered where to put myself. I never liked being near the door because of the draft, and the back of the tent often got a little cold too. I decided to chance it and take a spot in the middle, hoping that my fellow campers wouldn't keep me awake by snoring or making a fuss.

I gave my kit a final check as the first three tent mates arrived. They looked sound enough and didn't cause a ruckus as they chose their spots.

My heart sank when I heard the sound of laughter, looked up, and saw the three guys from Macau walking in.

Even though it was summer, the temperature was noticeably colder when the sun started to set. The local mayor gave a speech that I couldn't understand, but the display of Mongolian dancing and high-speed horse riding was enough to keep me occupied for a while. Some of the runners were sitting around, eating their evening meals, but I wandered around. I got sidetracked looking at Tommy Chen's film crew, but soon enough I was thinking about getting back to the tent. When people started asking one another what type of shoes they were running in, how much their bags weighed, or whether they'd brought any extra supplies, it was definitely my cue to leave. Getting involved in those kinds of conversations on the day before a race starts is never a good idea. The minute you encounter someone who is doing something different, you'll end up doubting yourself.

I checked my watch—six thirty. Time to eat. Even though waiting can be hard when I'm nervous and it's dark already, I always make sure I eat at the right time the night before each day's race. You don't want to eat too early and have your body consuming the calories before you're actually running.

I got my food, climbed into my sleeping bag, and ate in silence in the tent.

I made sure I was asleep before anyone else came back.

3

PEOPLE ALWAYS GET UP WAY TOO EARLY ON the first day of these races. Their nerves get the best of them, and two or three hours before the start, the camp is buzzing with people packing and repacking their bags, eating their food, talking, and worrying about whether they've packed their bags right and eaten the right amount of breakfast at just the right time.

I get it. I've been there myself. But that's not how I operate anymore. I have a routine that's tried and tested.

Start minus ninety minutes—wake up, get dressed, visit toilets.

Start minus sixty minutes—keep warm in tent, eat high-calorie breakfast.

Start minus fifteen minutes—pack up sleeping bag and inflatable mattress, leave tent, and join start line.

To anyone watching, however, the last hour of my routine looks a little weird. I stay in my sleeping bag right up until it's time to leave, even when I'm eating my can of All Day Breakfast. While everyone else is hopping up and down outside, having eaten their dehydrated meals, I'm curled up in my bag, beanie hat pulled tight over my head, tucking into a cold can of beans, sausage, bacon, and mushrooms. I get a few looks because no multi-stage runner in their right mind would ever carry canned food; it's just not worth the weight. But I take just one can that I eat before the race starts, and the 450 calories are more than worth the bemused stares as people wonder what kind of amateur I am.

It tastes especially good knowing that for the next six days I'm going to be eating nothing but cold, rehydrated meals that taste like salmon or Bolognese-flavoured pasta, the occasional strip of biltong—dried and cured meat from South Africa—a few nuts, and dozens of energy gels. I'll be sick of this food before the end of the week, but it's lightweight nutrition that keeps my bag weight down.

I savoured every cold mouthful. I couldn't see the three Macau boys anywhere, but I could tell that the rest of my tent mates—two Brits and one American—were staring at me like I was a fool who was way out of his depth. Nobody said anything, and once I'd eaten, I lay back down and curled up as tight as I possibly could in my bag. I guessed they were probably still staring.

With a quarter hour left, I climbed out of the sleeping bag, packed my things away in my rucksack, and headed for the line. People stared as I knew they would. They always do when they see me coming on the first day. My skin-tight running top is bright yellow and covered in my sponsor's logo. And because I'm tall and skinny, I look like a banana. While confident in my pre-race preparation and training, I always start to question myself, seeing the start line. As much as I try to avoid it, I end up thinking the other runners look better than I do. They all seem to be fitter, stronger, and look more like endurance athletes while I suddenly feel like an amateur again. The only way through it is to clench my jaw, hide behind my sunglasses, and tell myself it's time to get down to business.

For a lot of runners, the act of lacing up their shoes, heading out the door, and letting their lungs and their legs find their perfect rhythm as they run through nature is a beautiful thing. It's about freedom, peace, and the moment when all time seems to stop and the stresses of daily life fade.

I'm not one of those runners. My wife is. Lucja runs because she loves running. She races because she loves the camaraderie and the sense of community. Not me. I don't love running. I don't really like it either. But I do love racing. I love competing.

It took me thirty-seven years to realize that racing was for me. For most of my teens and twenties, I played competitive cricket and hockey. Right from the start I loved the action of a well-bowled ball, a perfectly struck cover drive, and a rocket of a shot that sails into the top right corner of the goal. To me, both of those sports have the potential to fill me with the kind of peace and happiness that Lucja describes when she runs. But even though I could master the technical aspects of hitting and bowling, I never could deal with the dynamics of playing as part of a team. I've watched myself fly off into a rage at my underperforming teammates so many times during matches that I know I'm more of a solo sport kind of guy.

I played golf for a while and got pretty good too—good enough to hustle the weekend players on courses throughout the western suburbs of Sydney and come back home with enough money so Lucja and I could eat for the rest of the week. But there was something about the pressure and the need to fit in with all those etiquette rules that riled me. After I threw one too many tantrums and broke one too many putters, I finally decided that golf was not for me either.

When it came to running, I discovered, quite by accident, that my competitive side returned. We had moved out of London and were living in Manchester at the time. It was New Year's Eve, and I was listening to a friend from cricket go on and on about how he was going to take part in a half marathon in the spring. Dan was talking about bringing down his personal best of 1 hour 45 minutes. Thanks to Lucja, I knew enough about running to know that was an okay time, not amazing but better than a lot of people could run. Dan was quite fit as well, so I reckoned he was probably right in feeling confident about becoming a bit faster.

But he was just so cocky about it all. So I put down my beer and spoke up.

"I reckon I could beat you."

Dan laughed. The music was loud, and he had to lean in to make sure he'd heard correctly. "You what?"

"I could take you. Easy."

"You're not a runner, Dion. No way."

"Dan, I'm so confident I'll even give you five minutes."

The conversation got a bit wild after that. People were laughing and shouting, and pretty soon the deal was done. If I didn't beat Dan by five minutes, I'd take him, his wife, and Lucja out for dinner. If I won, he'd be the one paying.

Lucja gave me the kind of look that said, *Here we go again.* I just smiled back and held up my hands. As far as I was concerned, I'd just won a free sumptuous meal for the two of us.

The race was at the end of March, and I knew I had a double mountain to climb. I'd been running for a year or two, but never farther than two or three miles at a time; any more than that and I'd just get bored and fed up. I've always hated running when it's cold or wet—and Manchester in January and February serves up nothing but cold and wet. So a few weeks went by, and my training had barely begun.

Dan is one of those runners who can't resist coming back from a run and posting his times on Twitter. It wasn't long before his overconfidence began to show, and when I started to read how far he was running and how fast he was getting there, I had all the motivation I needed to get off the sofa and hit the streets. I knew that as long as I pushed myself to run farther and faster than the times Dan was posting, I'd be able to beat him.

I lined up alongside Dan and Lucja at the start line. Dan was looking fit and up for it. Lucja was loving the pre-race-hype and crowd-warm-up routine from the announcer whose job it was to get everyone pumped for the race start. I was feeling out of place among the thousands of other runners who all had what looked like better sports equipment than I had.

"You know I have very expensive taste in wine, Dion," Dan said. "You're going to need a second mortgage to pay for the meal tonight."

I didn't say anything. Just smiled.

"Seriously, mate," he said, looking genuinely concerned. "Are you all right for this? It feels hot already. Don't push yourself harder than you should."

I was feeling nervous. My mouth was dry, and it was all I could do to suck as much air as I possibly could into my lungs.

The gun was fired, and we were off. Dan was at my side, and we were going at a fair pace already. Lucja dropped back, and the two of us carried on together. He seemed strong and in control. I felt fine about keeping pace with him, happy that we were finally under way.

When we passed the first mile marker, it hit me that I had only twelve more in which to gain five minutes on Dan. So I did the only thing I could think of. I decided to give it everything I had, running as hard and as fast as I could. Pretty soon my lungs were in agony, and I felt as if there wasn't enough air in the sky to keep me going. I wanted to slow down just a little and recover, but I forced myself to keep up the pace. Those five minutes were going to come my way only if I kept pulling away from Dan.

Never once did I look back. Somehow I knew it wouldn't help. If I saw him close, I'd probably panic, and if he was too far back already, I might end up slowing down. I knew that the race was going to be won or lost in my head. If I kept focus and pushed on, I'd avoid distraction.

Dan was right about it being a hot day. I'd never experienced heat like it at that time of year in Manchester before, and all through the morning the noise of the crowd was broken up by the sound of ambulance sirens as they raced to help exhausted runners.

For me, though, the heat wasn't a threat. It was like a welcome friend. It reminded me of my childhood in Australia. I'd spend hours on summer days playing cricket or riding my bike in temperatures pushing up to 110 and 120 degrees. It wasn't anywhere near that hot during the race, but all the same I found myself getting stronger as the heat increased and the miles passed by.

At least I did until mile eleven. That's when I started to feel myself slowing down. My legs were numb and weak, as if someone had stripped half the muscles from them. But I kept running, pushing hard and reminding myself what was at stake: my pride.

I crossed the line in 1:34, a respectable time for a first-ever half marathon, and nine minutes faster than Dan's previous personal best. Was it going to be enough? He'd set off pretty fast, and his training had put him in line to beat it. All I could do was crouch at the finish, feel my lungs begin to recover, and watch the clock tick by and hope not to see him.

It was Lucja who crossed a little more than five minutes after me. We high-fived each other and smiled as we waited the best part of another ten minutes for Dan to finally come home.

"What happened?" he said once he had recovered a little. "You just sped off. You must have done more training than you let on."

I smiled and gave him a pat on the back. "You need to get off Twitter, mate."

The start line at the race was much like any other start line at any other race around the world; everyone doing their own thing to cope with the nerves. I was at the side, second or third row back from the front, trying to distract myself by looking at the others around me. Tommy Chen was there, looking focused and pretty damn good. He had his camera crew to the side and plenty of fans among the pack. "Good luck, Tommy," someone called out. "Hope you smash it!"

"Yeah, thanks," he said, shifting his feet back and forth. I watched as the smile fell quickly from his face. He was just as nervous as the rest of us. Maybe more so. I knew he was one of the up-and-coming stars of multi-stage ultras, but he'd come in second in the first of the five races the organizers hosted that year. The pressure was on him to deliver.

To keep myself busy for another minute or so, I did one more final check of my kit, making sure the straps were tight enough across my chest, the food I needed during the stage was in the correct pockets, and my bright yellow gaiters were covering my shoes properly. I knew we'd be running up a sand dune pretty soon in the day, and the last thing I wanted was to spend the four or five hours that followed with pieces of grit irritating my feet, which could possibly lead to blisters and other foot issues.

The start horn sounded, and what little noise there was from the small crowd disappeared from my world. The race began on a wide stretch of grass, and as we got under way, the usual crush of people was surging down the middle. You get all sorts wanting to take the lead on that first day, and I don't mind so much. That's the beauty of these races—even though world-class athletes are lining up alongside happy amateurs, there is no sense of hierarchy or rank. If you want to run at the front and can keep up the pace, then be my guest.

I had guessed that the start would be a little bit tricky, with the runners bunching up as they usually did, so I'd put myself far out wide of everyone else. I didn't want to be tripped off the line, and if I went off fast enough, I could get ahead of the slower runners before the course narrowed and dropped down into a rocky canyon.

My plan worked as I soon fell in closely behind Tommy after the first 100 meters. It hadn't been raining in the night, but the rocks were slippery from the morning dew. I struggled to keep my footing and felt a bit uneasy and took it steady, just like Tommy. I guess we both knew that if we put a foot down wrong and twisted an ankle, we'd have no choice but to put up with a whole lot of pain for another 150 miles or, worse yet, a Did Not Finish.

I heard someone move up behind me and watched as a Romanian guy flew right past me. He was skipping over the rocks as if they were mini trampolines. Once Tommy knew he was behind him, both of them pulled away from me a little. *Keep it steady*, I told myself. *No need to worry.* I had put together a detailed stage-by-stage race plan with my coach before I'd left Scotland. We'd looked back at my other races and noticed that I'd been making the same mistake a lot of the time.

I tended to start slowly and then make up ground as the week went on, particularly on the long day, which had become one of my strengths, when the stage typically covered fifty miles or more. The truth is that I'm just not a morning person, and the first morning of them all always seems to hit me hard. I've often found myself twenty minutes down on the race leaders at the end of day one, which makes it close to impossible to make back up.

Even in training runs I struggle to get going, and for the first mile or two, I always question whether I want to keep going. I spend those first few minutes feeling like I'd rather be doing anything other than running. But if I push through it, I'm usually fine, and during the last half of a run, I'll be flying.

I trusted that as long as I kept Tommy and this Romanian guy in my sights, I'd be all right. If I was close at the end of stage one, keeping pace but not overcooking, I'd be putting myself in the best possible position for the rest of the week.

Halfway through the day, when the Romanian started to tire

and fell back so far behind us that I could no longer hear him, I looked up and saw a sand dune towering up ahead. It was steep and wide, easily three hundred feet high. I'd seen dunes like it in Morocco, but this one seemed different somehow. The sand on the side looked harder and more compact, but the path I had to run up was soft and offered almost no resistance at all.

There's a key to running up a sand dune, and I learned it the hard way back when I first competed in the Marathon des Sables. I didn't know that you have to keep your stride as short as you possibly can, ensuring a quick cadence to avoid the sand breaking underneath your feet and slowing you down. I didn't know that sometimes the longer path is easier than the shorter one. As a result, I tanked and came in so late at the end of the first day that I was seriously considering dropping out altogether.

Tommy attacked the dune ahead of me, but after just a couple of strides it was obvious that sand in the Gobi Desert was not like the Saharan stuff. It must have rained in the area overnight, and the sand was darker, clumpier. It gave way with the slightest pressure, falling away like weak clay, and at times I had to use my hands to gain a little extra grip. We weren't running up it; we were scrambling.

Once we were finally at the top, I could see the dune more clearly. The only option was to run along the narrow peak that stretched ahead for almost a mile. On both sides, the dune fell away, and if anyone put a foot wrong, he'd end up falling all the way down to the bottom. It would take ages to clamber back up, wasting precious time and precious energy.

Tommy was loving it. "Look at this view!" he shouted. "Isn't it magnificent?"

I said nothing back. I'm scared of heights and was terrified that I'd fall. I moved ahead as cautiously as I could. More than once my foot slipped, and I threw my arms out in a desperate attempt to regain my balance. At that point I didn't particularly care how much ground Tommy made on me. All I could do was stare at where my feet were heading and hope that the sand held.

As much as I hated being on top of the dune, when it came time to run down it, I was in heaven. I put a bit of power into my legs and sprinted down as fast as I could. By the time I hit bottom, I overtook Tommy. I felt his surprise and heard him keeping close behind me.

We ran side by side for a while, until the Romanian caught back up with us, and then the three of us traded the lead from time to time. The course took us through muddy fields and over bridges, alongside a giant reservoir. The vast sands and cruel heat of the Gobi Desert were a couple of days away, and we ran through remote villages that belonged in another century. Tumbledown buildings squatted on the land like an abandoned movie set. Occasionally we'd see locals, standing and staring impassively at us. They never said anything, but they didn't seem bothered by us either. It wouldn't have made any difference to me either way. I was flying by this time, full of hope that the race in the Gobi Desert might not be my last race after all.

4

I WAS BORN IN SYDNEY, NEW SOUTH WALES, but grew up in an Australian outback town in Queensland called Warwick. It's a place that barely anyone I meet has visited but one that contains the kind of people everyone can recognize. It's farming country, with traditional values and a strong emphasis on family. These days it's changed a lot and become a small, vibrant city, but when I was a teenager, Warwick was the kind of place that would fill up on a Friday night. The pubs would be crammed with hardworking men looking for a good night out involving a few too many beers, a couple of fights, and a trip to the petrol station—which any self-respecting Australian calls the 'servo'—for a meat pie that had been kept in a warmer all day and was hard as a rock.

They were good people, but it was a cliquish town at the time, and everyone knew everyone else's business. I knew I didn't belong among them.

It wasn't just the scandal of my abnormal childhood and family situation that prompted people to react badly. It was the way I behaved. It was who I had become. I went from being a polite, pleasant little kid to an awkward, pain-in-the-ass loudmouth. By the time I was fourteen, I was the class joker, riling the teachers with my crowd-pleasing comments, getting thrown out of class, and swaggering my way out of the school gates as I walked to the servo for an early afternoon pie while the other fools were still stuck in class.

And when my school year ended and the headmaster greeted each of us with a handshake and a friendly word about our futures at the final assembly, all he could say to me was, "I'll be seeing you in prison."

Of course, there was a reason for all this, and it wasn't just the pain of losing my dad—not just once but twice over.

I was falling apart because everything at home seemed to me to be falling apart.

It seemed the loss of her husband hit my mum hard. Really hard. Her own father had returned from the Second World War traumatized, and like so many men, he turned to alcohol to numb the pain. Mum's childhood taught her that when parents are struggling, home isn't always the best place to be.

So when Mum became a widow in her early thirties with two young children, she coped the only way she knew how. She retreated. I remember days going by with her being locked in the bedroom. I cooked meals of eggs on toast or spaghetti out of a can, or else we went to Nan's, some other neighbour's house, or, if it was Sunday, church.

From what I could see, Mum would go through phases where she became fixated with keeping the house immaculate. She cleaned relentlessly, and on the odd occasion that she did cook for herself, she'd clean the kitchen frantically for two hours. Neither I nor my little sister, Christie, could do anything right. Kids being kids, if we'd leave crumbs around the place, smear our finger marks on windows, or take showers that lasted longer than three minutes, it might upset her.

Ours was a half-acre, filled with trees and flower beds. While Mum and Dad used to love working in it together, after Dad's death it was up to me to get out and keep it tidy. If I didn't do my chores, I felt life wasn't worth living.

When Mum would start nagging at me, pretty soon she'd be yelling at me and screaming. "You're useless," she'd say. I'd scream and yell back, and soon we both would be swearing at each other. Mum never apologized. Nor did I. But we both had said things we'd later regret.

We argued endlessly, every day and every night. I'd come home from school and feel like I had to walk on eggshells around the house. If I made any noise or disturbed her in any way, the whole fighting thing would start up again.

By the time I was fourteen, she'd had enough. "You're out," she said one day as, following yet another storm of mutually hurled insults, she pulled out cleaning supplies from the cupboard. "There's too much arguing, and nothing you do is right. You're moving downstairs."

The house was a two-storey home, but everything that mattered was upstairs. Downstairs was the part of the house where nobody ever went. It was where Christie and I played when we were little, but since then the playroom had become a dumping ground. There was a toilet down there, but barely any natural light, and a big area that was still full of building supplies. Most important for my mum, there was a door at the base of the stairway that could be locked. Once I was down there, I felt trapped, stopped from being part of the family life above.

I didn't argue with her. Part of me wanted to get away from her.

So I moved my mattress and my clothes and settled into my new life—a new life in which Mum would open the door when it was time for me to come up and get food or when I needed to go to school. Apart from that, if I was at home, I was confined to the basement.

The thing I hated most about it was not the fact that I felt like some kind of a prisoner. What I hated about it was the dark.

Soon after Garry's death, I started sleepwalking. It got worse when I moved down, and I would wake up in the area where all the broken tiles were dumped. It'd be pitch black; I'd be terrified and unable to figure out which way to turn to switch on the lights. Everything became frightening, and my dreams would fill with nightmare images of Freddy Krueger waiting for me outside my room.

Most nights, as I listened to the lock turn, I'd fall on my bed and sob into the stuffed Cookie Monster toy I'd had since I was a kid.

Normally I don't take a mattress with me on a race, but I was worried my leg injury might flare up at some point crossing the Gobi Desert, so I'd packed one specially. I blew it up at the end of the first day and tried to rest up. I had a little iPod with me, but I didn't bother putting it on. I was fine with just lying back and thinking about the day's race. I was happy with third place, especially as there was only a minute or two between me, Tommy, and the Romanian, whose name I later found out was Julian.

Instead of an army surplus tent, we were in a yurt that night, and I was looking forward to its being good and warm as the temperature dropped. Meanwhile, though, I guessed I'd have to wait a while before any of my tent mates returned. I ate a little biltong and curled up in my sleeping bag.

It took an hour or so before the first two guys arrived back. I was dozing when I first became aware of them talking, and I heard one of my tent mates, an American named Richard, say, "Whoa! Dion's back already!" I looked up, smiled, and said hi and congratulated them on finishing the first stage.

Richard went on to say he was planning on speaking with the three Macau guys as soon as they got in. I'd slept all through the first night, but according to Richard, they'd been up late messing with their bags and up early talking incessantly.

I wasn't worried too much, and thinking about Lucja and how she'd got me into running in the first place, I drifted back to sleep.

I first tried running when we were living in New Zealand. Lucja was managing an eco-hotel, and I was working for a wine exporter. Life was good, and the days of having to hustle the golf courses for food money were behind us. Even better, both our jobs came with plenty of perks, such as free crates of wine and great meals out. Every night we'd put away a couple of bottles of wine, and on weekends we'd eat out. We'd take Curtly, our Saint Bernard (named after legendary West Indian cricketer Curtly Ambrose), out for a walk in the morning, stopping off at a café for sweet potato corn fritters or a full fry-up of eggs, bacon, sausage, beans, mushrooms, tomato, and toast. We might get a pastry on the way home, crack open a bottle of something at lunch, then head out in the evening for a three-course meal with more wine. Later we'd walk Curtly one more time and get an ice cream.

People would tell me I was a big lad, and they were right. I weighed 240 pounds and was heavier than I had ever been in my life. I didn't do any exercise, was an off-again on-again smoker, and had created a dent in the sofa where I lay and watched sports on TV. I was twenty-six and eating myself to death.

The change came when Lucja made some new friends who loved running and fitness. She got onto her own health kick and started slimming down. She explained that she wanted to look good in a bikini, and I—like a typical guy from my part of the world—told her she was being ridiculous.

But I didn't believe what I said. I knew she was made of strong stuff, that she was determined and was going to see this through.

Lucja quickly got into running and found that she was completing her three-mile loop faster and faster.

"You're so unfit and unhealthy, Bubba," she said, calling me by the name I was now beginning to dislike. "I could beat you."

I was lying on the sofa at the time, watching cricket. "Don't be stupid. I could beat you easily. You've only been at it for six weeks."

In my mind, I was still a sportsman. I was the same kid who could spend all day playing cricket or running about with his friends. Besides, I had something that Lucja lacked—a killer competitive instinct. I'd competed so much as a teenager and won so many matches that I was convinced I could still beat her at any challenge she threw at me.

I found some shorts and tennis shoes, stepped over Curtly, who was sleeping on the front step, and joined Lucja on the street outside.

"You sure you're ready for this, Bubba?"

I snorted in disbelief. "Are you kidding? There's no way you're winning."

"All right then. Let's go."

We kept pace—for the first fifty feet. After that, Lucja started pulling away from me. My brain was demanding that I keep up, but it was impossible. I had nothing to give. I was like an old steamroller whose fire had gone out, gradually getting slower and slower.

By the time I'd covered another hundred feet, I stopped moving altogether. Up ahead, the road made a slight turn and went up a hill. The defeat felt heavy within me.

I stood bent over, hands on knees, retching, coughing, and gasping for breath. I looked up to see Lucja way ahead of me. She looked back at me for a second, then carried on running up the hill.

I was enraged. How could I get beaten? I turned around and walked back home. With each step, the anger was joined by something else. Panic.

The healthier she became and the more weight she lost, the greater my risk of losing her. On the day of the run, I knew she wouldn't stop, that this wasn't just a phase or a passing fad. She was determined, and I knew she'd keep going until she was happy. And when she reached that point, why would she stay with a fat bloke like me?

I woke up again but this time to the sound of the Macau boys coming back into the tent. They were all pumped up at having completed the first stage and were spreading out their kits, looking for their evening meals. That was when Richard pulled off his headphones and started talking to them in what sounded to me like perfect Mandarin.

Judging by their reaction, they understood every word he said, and they were taking it seriously. They looked like schoolboys being told off, not knowing where to look. As Richard was finishing, he pointed at me. They all stared in silence, grabbed their food from their bags, and slipped out of the tent.

"What did you say?" asked Allen, one of the British guys in the tent.

"I told them that tonight they had to be quiet and more organized. They've got to get their stuff organized before dinner, come back, and rest. That guy's here to win."

They all turned and looked at me.

"Is he right?" asked Allen. "Are you here to win?"

"Well, yes," I said. "I'm not here for fun, if that's what you mean."

Richard laughed. "We got that impression. You're not exactly sociable, are you?"

I laughed too. I liked this guy.

"Yeah, some of that's because I'm cold, and some of it's just how I get through these races." I paused. "But thanks for saying that to them."

It was six thirty in the evening when I shuffled out of my sleeping bag and wandered outside the yurt carrying a bag of dehydrated whatever-it-was I was going to eat that night. While we have to carry all our own food, bedding, and clothes on a multi-stage ultra, at least our water is provided. I found the fire where water was being boiled and made up a chilli con carne–flavoured meal. It tasted pretty bland, just like it always did, but I reminded myself I wasn't there for fun. It had the bare minimum calories I required to keep going, and I needed to eat every last bit of it.

Everyone was sitting around the fire and chatting. I liked the idea of resting in its glow and soaking up the heat for a while, but all the seats were taken, so I crouched down on an uncomfortable rock and ate. After scooping the very last traces of food from the corners of the bag, I headed back to the yurt. It had been a good day—a really good one, in fact—but I'd need a solid night's sleep and an equally good day tomorrow to keep my number three slot. I'd started the day as an unknown. I guessed that from now on people would be a bit more aware of me in the race. And that could make things difficult.

It was when I got up that I saw a dog. It was maybe a foot tall and sandy coloured with great dark eyes and a funny-looking mustache and beard. It was walking around between the chairs, getting up on its hind legs and charming people into giving it bits of food. Getting runners to part with any of their food this early in the race was no mean feat.

Clever dog, I thought. *There's no way I'd feed it.*

PART 2

5

THE YURT HAD BEEN SO HOT I'D BARELY BEEN able to sleep all night, but as I walked out the next morning, the air was cold enough to make me shiver. The ground was wet, and the Tian Shan up ahead appeared to be covered in low dark clouds that were surely going to dump more rain on us.

With a few minutes to go before the eight o'clock start, I took my place on the start line at the front of the pack. After coming in third yesterday, I felt as though I belonged there.

People were a lot less nervous than before. I could even hear some of them laughing, though I tried my best to block out all distractions and focus on the challenge ahead. I knew we'd face mile after mile of ascent as we headed up into the mountains, followed by some dangerous descents. We were already at an altitude of seven thousand feet, and I guessed that some runners would already be struggling with the lack of oxygen. Today was going to make things harder by taking us up to more than nine thousand feet.

My concentration was broken by the sound of more laughter and a little cheering behind me.

"It's the dog!"

"How cute!"

I looked down and saw the same dog from last night. It was standing by my feet, staring at the bright yellow gaiters covering my shoes. It was transfixed for a while, its tail wagging constantly. Then it did the strangest thing. It looked up, its dark black eyes taking in my legs first, then my yellow-shirted torso, and finally my face. It looked right into my eyes, and I couldn't look away.

"You're cute," I said under my breath, "but you'd better be fast if you're not planning to get trodden by one hundred runners chasing after you."

I looked about to see if anyone was going to come and claim the dog and get it out of the way before the runners took off. A few other runners caught my eye, smiled, and nodded at the dog, but none of the locals or the race staff seemed to notice.

"Does anyone know whose dog this is?" I asked, but nobody did. They were all too focused on the ten-second countdown to the race start.

"Nine . . . eight . . . seven . . ."

I looked down. The dog was still at my feet, only now it had stopped staring at me and was sniffing my gaiters.

"You'd better get away little doggie, or else you're going to get squashed."

"Five . . . four . . ."

"Go on," I said, trying to get it to move. It was no use. It took a playful bite of the gaiter, then jumped back and crouched on the ground before diving in for another sniff and a chew.

The race began, and as I set off, the dog came with me. The gaiters game was even more fun now that the gaiters moved, and the dog danced around my feet as if it was the best fun ever.

It seemed to me that the cute moment could become annoying if it carried on for too long. The last thing I wanted was to trip over the little pooch and cause injury to it or myself. Then again, I knew there was a long stretch of single track coming up in which it would be hard to overtake a lot of the slower runners, so I wanted to keep up the pace and not lose my position with the front runner.

I was thankful when, after a quarter mile, I looked back down and saw that the dog wasn't there. *Probably gone back to its owner at the camp*, I thought.

The track narrowed, and we entered a flat forest section that lasted a few miles. I was in second, a few feet behind a Chinese guy I'd not seen before. Every once in a while he'd miss a marker—a pink paper square about the size of a CD case attached to a thin metal spike in the ground. They were hard to miss, and in the forest sections there was one of them every ten or twenty feet.

"Hey!" I'd shout on the couple of occasions that he took a wrong turn and headed off into the forest. I'd wait for him to track back, then fall in again behind him. I guess I could have let him keep going or shouted my warning and then carried on running, but multi-stage runners have a certain way of doing things. If we're going to beat someone, we want it to be because we're faster and stronger, not because we've tricked them or refused to help when we could. After all, pushing our bodies as hard as we do, everyone makes mistakes from time to time. You never know when you're going to need someone to help you out.

The forest fell away as the path started its climb into the mountains. I kept up the six-minute-mile pace, concentrating on keeping my stride short and my feet quick. My body remembered the hours I'd spent with my coach standing beside the treadmill, beating out the rapid cadence to which he wanted me to run. His shouts of "one-two-three-one-two-three" were like torture at first, but after a few sessions of spending a whole hour running like that, three minutes on then one minute off, my legs finally got the message. If I wanted to run fast and not feel the crippling pain anymore, I had no choice but to learn how to run this way.

I saw something move out of the corner of my eye and forced myself to look down for a fraction of a second. It was the dog again. It wasn't interested in my gaiters this time but, instead, seemed happy just to trot along beside me.

Weird, I thought. *What's it doing here?*

I pressed on and attacked the incline. Zeng, the Chinese guy who was leading, is an accomplished ultra-runner and had pulled away from me a little. I couldn't hear anyone behind me. It was just me and the dog, side by side, tearing into the switchbacks. The path was interrupted by a man-made culvert. It was only three feet wide, and I didn't think anything of it, leaping over the fast-flowing water without breaking stride.

I could tell the dog had stayed behind. It started barking, then making a strange whimpering sound. I didn't turn back to look. I never do. Instead, I kept my head in the race and pushed on. As far as I knew, the dog belonged to someone back near the camp. The little thing had had a pretty good workout for the day, conned some runners out of some high-calorie food, and now it was time to head home.

I was fifteen when I told my mum I was leaving the dingy basement and moving in with a friend. She barely said anything. It seemed to me she didn't care. I guess since I'd already been staying with friends whenever I could—and the fact that when I was around, Mum and I fought endlessly, trading insults like boxers at a weigh-in—it couldn't have come as much of a surprise. In fact, it was probably a relief.

I moved in with a guy named Deon. "Dion and Deon?" said the woman who ran the hostel when Deon introduced me. "You're kidding, right?"

"No," said Deon. "Straight up."

She snorted and turned away mumbling. "I've heard it all now."

Deon was a year older than me, had left school already, and was an apprentice bricklayer. He'd had his own troubles at home.

Even though we were both finally free from the struggles at home, neither of us was too excited about life in the hostel. The walls were paper-thin, and everyone else living there was older and freaked us out. The hostel was filled with homeless people, travellers, and drunks. Food was always going missing from the communal areas, and barely a night went by without the whole hostel waking up to the sound of a fight breaking out.

While I was still at school, I also took a part-time job pumping petrol at the servo. It brought a little bit of money in but not enough, and I had to rely on Deon to help with the shortfall each week.

I only just managed to keep up with my schoolwork, but none of my teachers showed any sign of caring about where I was living or how I was coping with life away from home. In fact, I don't think any of them knew about my new living arrangements, and I wanted to keep it that way. I was embarrassed to go back to the hostel and tried to hide the truth from my classmates with their perfect, loving family homes.

Deon was the kind of guy who could charm the birds from the trees. We'd sneak into the pub on a Friday or Saturday night, have a few beers, and try to chat up some girls. I'd let Deon do the talking, much like I'd let him do the dancing. Aussie blokes from towns like mine didn't dance in those days, and it was almost inevitable that when he finally came off the dance floor, Deon would take a mouthful of abuse and a few thrown punches. He'd just laugh them off.

One Sunday afternoon as we lay on our bunks wasting time, we heard shouting in the corridor outside. Someone was calling Deon's name, saying he was going to kill him for sleeping with his girlfriend.

The two of us froze. I stared at Deon, who looked for the first time ever genuinely scared for his life. We both tried to act tough when we were in the hostel, but we were just kids—who at that moment were terrified we were about to get our heads kicked in. Luckily the blokes didn't know which room we were in, and they kept moving up and down the corridor until they eventually left. That was enough of a shock to get us to move out of the hostel as soon as possible.

The Grand Hotel was a step up from the hostel, but it wasn't much of a hotel. It was just a pub with a few rented rooms at the top. Instead of addicts, drunks, and homeless blokes, the Grand was home to guys who worked on the railroad or in the local meat-packing plant. One was an ex-pro pool player who had once beaten the national champion but had drunk all his talent away. Another was a traveller who had run out of money and simply decided to make Warwick his home. I liked listening to him talk. "Any place can be all right," he'd say, "as long as you accept what's wrong with it."

I felt much happier at the Grand than I did at the hostel. I liked being in the company of the kind of people who had chosen their lot and were happy with it, even if it meant not having the perfect wife, the perfect house, and the perfect family. I felt free living among them, and for the first time in years, it seemed to me that all the things my mum had said that made me feel worthless and unwanted, an unlovable screw-up and a disappointment, might not necessarily be true. Maybe I could learn to get by after all.

The barking and whimpering continued until I was twenty feet past the culvert. Then there was silence. I had a moment of hoping the dog hadn't fallen into the water, but before I could think about it much more, there was a familiar flash of brown beside me. The dog was back by my side again.

You're a determined little thing, aren't you?

Soon the track became even steeper as the temperature dropped lower. The cold air had numbed my face and fingers, but I was sweating. The increase in altitude made my breathing tight and my head a little dizzy. If I was going to run without stopping all the way up the mountain, I knew I'd have to dig in even more than usual.

I hate mountain running. Even though I live in Edinburgh and am surrounded by the beauty of the Scottish Highlands, I avoid running outside and up hills whenever possible. Especially when it's wet, cold, and windy. But give me a desert baked in 110-degree heat, and I'll be as happy as any runner out there.

People often ask me why I like running in the heat so much. The answer is simple: I've always felt the most freedom when I'm running beneath a blazing sun.

It started when I was a kid. After Garry died, I turned to sport in the hope of finding refuge from the troubles at home. I'd spend hours outside playing cricket or hockey. Time would stop when I was outside, and the more I ran and pushed myself, the heavier my breathing became, and the louder my heart beat, the quieter the sadness and sorrow grew within me.

Maybe you could say that running in the heat was a form of escape. What I do know for sure is that as I ran in the Gobi Desert, I was no longer running to get away from my past. I was running towards my future. I was running with hope, not sorrow.

My pace slowed as every step became its own battle. There was snow all around, and at one point the track ran alongside a glacier. At other times the mountain would drop away at the side. I guessed there were some pretty dramatic views this high up, but I was thankful the cloud was so low that it was impossible to see anything more than a thick wall of grey mist. The experience was surreal, and I couldn't wait for it to be over.

The checkpoint finally came into view, and I heard people call out the usual encouragement. Once they saw the dog, they shouted a little louder.

"There's that dog again!"

I'd almost forgotten the little dog at my side. All the time that I'd been struggling up the hill, the dog had kept pace with me, skipping along as if running 2,500 feet up into the sky was the most natural thing in the world.

Once I was at the checkpoint, I faced the usual range of questions about how I was feeling and whether I had been drinking my water. Checkpoints are there to give runners an opportunity to refill their water bottles, but they're also a chance for the race team to check us over and make sure we are fit to carry on.

This time, however, it was the dog who got far more attention than me. A couple of volunteers took some photos as the dog sniffed about the checkpoint tent. As soon as my bottles were full and I was ready to go, I moved out, half expecting this might be the point when the dog decided to leave me in favour of a better meal ticket.

But when I and my yellow gaiters started running out, the dog joined me straightaway.

If the climb to the top of the mountain had been tough, then the descent was its own unique sort of pain. For more than five miles the route took me straight down a path covered in rocks and loose stones. It was brutal on the joints, but like any runner, I knew that if I ran at anything less than 100 per cent, I'd get caught by whoever was behind me.

And that's exactly what happened. I was feeling sluggish and struggled to hit anything close to my maximum pace on the descent, and soon enough Tommy glided past me, quickly followed by Julian.

I was annoyed with myself for giving too much on the ascent. I'd made a basic error, the kind I knew better not to make.

I checked myself. Getting annoyed could lead me to make another basic error. At times in the past, I'd let myself obsess about a mistake I'd made. Over the course of a few miles, the frustration would build and build until I'd lose all interest in the race and bail out.

I tried to distract myself by concentrating on the view. Coming down from the mountain at one point, I thought I saw a giant lake ahead of us, stretched out wide and dark beneath the grey skies. The closer I got, the more it became clear that it wasn't a lake but a huge expanse of dark sand and gravel.

As the path flattened, I settled into a steady six-and-a-half-minute-per-mile pace, bursting through the final checkpoint, not bothering to stop for water. I saw Tommy, Zeng, and Julian up ahead and found they hadn't opened up the gap as much as I had feared. They were racing one another hard, and with less than a mile to go, there was no way for me to catch them. But I didn't mind so much. I felt good to be finishing strong without any hint of pain in my leg. I could hear the drums that played every time a runner crossed the finish line, and I knew that finishing a close fourth for the day would hopefully be enough to keep me in third overall.

Just as at each of the day's checkpoints, the dog was the focus of attention at the finish. People were taking pictures and filming, cheering for the little brown mutt as it crossed the line. The dog seemed to like the attention, and I could swear it was playing to the crowd by wagging its tail even faster.

Tommy had got in a minute or two before me, and he joined in the applause. "That dog, man! It's been following you all day!"

"Has it had any water?" asked one of the volunteers.

"I have no idea," I said. "Maybe it drank at some of the streams on the way." I felt a little bad about it. I didn't like the idea of its being thirsty or hungry.

Someone found a small bucket and gave the dog some water. It lapped it up, obviously thirsty.

I stepped back, wanting to leave the dog to it and get away from the crowds a little. Again I thought it might wander off and go find someone else to follow, but it didn't. As soon as it finished drinking, it looked up, locked eyes on my yellow gaiters, and trotted over to my side, following me wherever I went.

It was hot in the camp, and I was glad we'd left all that horrible alpine cold up in the mountains. From now on the race was going to be about coping with the heat, not struggling through the cold. From tomorrow onward we'd be in the Gobi Desert. I couldn't wait.

As soon as I sat down in the tent, the dog curled up next to me—and I started thinking about germs and diseases. It's crucial during a weeklong race to keep as clean as possible because without any access to showers or wash basins, it's easy to get sick from anything you touch. The dog was looking right into my eyes, just as it had earlier that morning. I had a few hours before my six-thirty meal, so I pulled out one of the packs of nuts and biltong. The dog's stare was unbreakable.

With a piece of meat midway to my mouth, it struck me that I hadn't seen the dog eat a thing all day. It had run the best part of a marathon, and still it wasn't trying to beg or steal any of the food I had in front of me.

"Here you go," I said, tossing half the meat down onto the tarpaulin in front of it, instinct telling me that feeding by hand wasn't a risk I wanted to take. The dog chewed, swallowed, spun around a few times, and lay down. Within seconds it was snoring, then twitching, then whimpering as it drifted deeper and deeper into sleep.

I woke up to the sound of grown men cooing like school kids.

"Ah, how cute is that?"

"Isn't that the dog from last night? Did you hear she followed him all day?"

She. The dog had run with me all day, and I'd never thought to check what sex it was.

I opened my eyes. The dog was staring right at me, looking deeper into my eyes than I would have thought possible. I checked. They were right. It wasn't an it. It was a she.

"Yeah," I said to Richard and the rest of the guys. "She stuck with me all day. She's got a good little motor on her."

Some of the guys fed her, and again she took whatever she was given, but gently. It was almost as though she knew she was getting a good deal here and she needed to be on her best behaviour.

I told the guys I'd been wondering where she came from and that I'd guessed she'd belonged to whoever owned the yurts we'd stayed in the previous night.

"I don't think so," said Richard. "I heard some of the other runners say she joined them out on the dune yesterday."

That meant she had put in almost fifty miles in two days. I was staggered.

It also meant she didn't belong to the people back at the previous camp or to one of the race organizers.

"You know what you've got to do now, don't you?" said Richard.

"What?"

"You've got to give her a name."

6

I STOPPED RUNNING LESS THAN A MILE IN AND cursed my stupidity.

The last twenty-four hours had brought all kinds of weather our way, from the snow and rain of the mountains to the dry heat that greeted us as we came down to camp. All night high winds had been tearing at the sides of the tent, and when I got up, the temperature was the coldest for any start yet.

The cold bothered me. I'd been looking forward to the day, knowing it was going to be flatter and hotter, but, instead, I'd found myself shivering on the start line. While the other runners went through their pre-race routines, I'd thrown off my backpack, rummaged around inside, and pulled out my light jacket, completely upsetting my usual precise and carefully prepared race start.

And now I was taking it off again. After a few minutes the sun had come out, and the temperature had started to rise. I should have been happy about it, but I could feel myself start to overheat in my wet weather gear. With five hours of hard running ahead of me, I had no choice but to stop.

As I pulled at zippers and plastic clips and shoved the jacket away, I noticed Tommy, Julian, and two others run past and reclaim the lead.

Then one more runner approached, and I smiled.

"Hey, Gobi," I said, using the name I'd given her the night before. "You changed your mind, did you?"

She'd spent the night curled up at my side, but once I got to the start line that morning, she'd disappeared among the crowd of other runners. I'd been too focused on the weather to worry about her. Besides, if the previous twenty-four hours had taught me anything, it was that she was a determined little thing. If she had other plans for her day, who was I to stop her?

But there was Gobi, looking up at me as I fastened my bag, then down at my gaiters. She was ready to go. So was I.

I pushed hard to catch up with the leaders and was soon tucked in behind them. I knew a long stretch of the race went through a section of large boulders, and I remembered how light on his feet Julian had been when we hit similar terrain the first day. I didn't like the thought of watching him skip away from me again, so I pushed my way up past the third and fourth runners, then overtook Julian and Tommy.

Being out in front again felt good. My legs felt strong, and my head was up. I could hear the gap between me and the other runners grow bigger with every minute that passed. I was able to run hard, and whenever I started to tire, all I needed to do was glance quickly down at Gobi. She didn't know anything about running technique or race strategy. She didn't even know how far I was planning on running throughout the day. She was running free, running because that was what she was made to do.

I followed the pink course markers all the way to the boulder section. The flat path I'd been on veered to the right, but the markers carried on straight ahead, through the rocks that looked big, unstable, and like they were going to make it almost impossible to keep up any kind of pace. But there was no avoiding them, and I scrambled up, feeling the smaller rocks shift and move beneath me as I went. I hoped I wasn't going to twist an ankle, and envied Gobi's ability to bound effortlessly over them.

I knew Julian was going to be quicker than me in this section, and as we approached the peak, I could hear him closing in behind me. But as I finally reached the top, instead of pushing ahead and trying to hold him off as long as I could, I froze.

I could see everything from up there. The checkpoint sat off in the distance, with a small village we would run through before it. I could see the way the boulder section sloped off ahead of us for another thousand feet, the pink race markers plotting the course as it returned to the flat path that led to the village, the checkpoint, and beyond.

None of that was what I was looking at.

My gaze, just like that of Julian and the other two runners who had pulled up alongside him, was firmly fixed on the solitary figure running off to the right.

It was Tommy.

"Whoa," said Julian. "Not right."

Tommy had somehow skipped the entire boulder section and gained a bit of time. By my calculations he'd made ten minutes on us.

All three of us were furious, but Tommy was too far ahead to hear us if we shouted. So we set off as a pack with renewed fire in our bellies, determined to catch him.

We could see Tommy at the checkpoint ahead as we ran through the village, but by the time we reached it ourselves, he had disappeared over a ridge a few hundred feet away.

I decided to pause long enough to raise the alarm and make

sure someone had a record of what happened. The member of the organizing team looked at me as if I was an idiot when I first tried to explain it.

"Say that again, please?" she said.

"Tommy Chen missed that whole rocky section back there. I don't know if he did it deliberately or not, but it's not fair."

"We'll look into it later," she said, giving me the brush-off.

"Tommy cut corner," said Zeng, who'd been with us and seen it all. "Not right."

Again, she didn't seem to care all that much. Soon we were back out of the checkpoint, trying to catch up with Tommy. He had almost a mile of tough terrain on us, but I had rage on my side. I pushed the pace up to a six-and-a-half-minute mile and worked hard to start reeling him in. Julian and the others stayed back a little, but I didn't mind. I was on a mission.

The path was undulating, and there were only a few times when I could see Tommy clearly. At one point there was only a half mile between us when he turned around, saw me running hard towards him, turned back, and sprinted off as fast as he possibly could.

I couldn't believe it.

There's an etiquette to these races. If you realize you've gained an unfair advantage over other runners, you hang back, let them catch up, and allow the proper order to be restored. I've made this kind of error myself in another race. It's easy to do in the battle for the lead, but it's better to settle while on the race course rather than after the run is completed.

I pressed on after him, but after working so hard to try to narrow the gap, and having let myself get so angry, I soon felt tired. I heard footsteps behind me, and Julian overtook me. The heat started to rise, and the race moved onto a long, flat road that extended off for miles into the distance. I started to feel bored, then frustrated with myself.

Previous experience had taught me that feeling this way was toxic. But it had also taught me how to deal with it.

In my first-ever ultra-race—a full marathon with a six-mile loop added onto the end—I'd started to feel tired at around the twenty-mile mark. By the time I approached it, I was done. I wasn't enjoying the running, and I was fed up with getting overtaken by men and women who were much older than me. I'd done it only to keep Lucja company, and even though I was about to complete the 26.2 miles in a respectable 3:30, I gave up inside. I stepped off the course, headed back to the car, and waited for Lucja to join me.

It took hours.

As I sat in the car and watched the rest of the field put in the hard work that I wasn't prepared to put in myself, I started to feel like I'd let myself down.

The field had thinned, and the only people still running were the kind of people who looked as if this event was a once-in-a-lifetime achievement. Lucja was fitter, faster, and stronger than all of them, and I was beginning to wonder what had happened. Eventually I got out of the car and walked back along the last mile of the course, looking for her. I found her soon enough, running slowly alongside a guy who obviously had a pretty serious leg injury. Lucja had struggled with fatigue toward the end of the race, but she had toughed it out.

I watched her cross the finish line and felt myself start to choke up. The mental strength and compassion Lucja showed that day has stayed with me ever since. I try to emulate her often when I'm racing, and at my best I can dig deep and tough out all kinds of pain and discomfort. But there are days when the voices calling me to quit shout louder than the voices calling me to keep on going. Those are the toughest days of all.

As I watched Julian disappear into the distance and tried not to think about how far ahead Tommy had gotten, I knew I was missing Lucja. But a quick glance down at Gobi was enough to bring back my focus and take my mind off the thing with Tommy. She was still beside me, still skipping along. Just by being there, Gobi made me want to keep going.

The long, flat section ended and gave way to scrubland. I'd noticed during the start of the stage that if Gobi saw a stream or puddle, she would occasionally run off to the side of the course and take a drink. Since the boulder section we'd not seen any water at all, and I wondered whether I might need to give her some of my own water. I didn't want to stop, but I was also starting to feel responsible for the dog's welfare. She wasn't a big dog, and her legs weren't much longer than my hands. All that running must have been hard on her.

So, initially at least, I was relieved when I saw the streams up ahead. Gobi trotted off and had a drink out of one of them, but if she'd been able to see what I could see, she wouldn't have been nearly so happy.

Beyond the stream I could see Julian, on the far side of a river that must have been at least 150 feet wide. I remembered that the organizers had spoken about it while I was shivering on the start line a few hours earlier. It was going to come up to my knees, but it was possible to walk across.

The sight of Julian spurred me on, and I didn't hesitate to wade in, checking that my bag was strapped on tight and high on my back. It was colder than I imagined, but I welcomed the chance to cool down a bit.

It was soon clear that the water was definitely going to reach my knees, and possibly even higher. The current was fast as well, and combined with the slippery rocks underfoot, I felt unsteady. I could handle continuing the race with wet shoes, for they'd dry out soon enough. But if I slipped, fell, and got my bag wet, not only would it become heavy and uncomfortable, but most of my food for the rest of the week would be ruined. One wrong foot, one tiny fall, and my race could be all over.

I was so focused on getting myself across that I didn't stop to think about Gobi. I guess I assumed that she'd find her own way across the river, just as she had with the culvert the day before.

This time, however, her barking and whining didn't stop. With every step I took, it became more desperate.

I was a quarter way across the river when I finally did what I had never done before in a race. I turned around.

She was on the bank, running up and down, looking right at me. I knew Julian was ahead by a few minutes, but I wondered how long it would be before someone came up behind me. If I went back, would I lose a place as well as valuable minutes?

I ran back as best I could, tucked her under my left arm, and waded back out into the cold water. I'd not picked her up before, and she was so much lighter than I imagined she would be. Even so, it was so much harder crossing with her. Using only my right arm for balance, I edged forward.

I slipped more than once, one time going down hard on my left side, getting Gobi and—I guessed—the bottom edge of my bag wet. But Gobi didn't complain, nor did she wriggle or try to escape. She stayed calm, letting me do my job and keep her safe.

I put her down when we reached a small island in the middle, and she trotted around as though the whole thing was a great adventure. Once I'd checked that my bag wasn't seriously wet and made sure it was as high up my back as I could get it, I called for Gobi, who immediately ran back to me. I scooped her up and continued on as before.

She scrambled up the bank on the other side a lot quicker than I did, and by the time I was clear of the mud and the undergrowth, Gobi had shaken herself off and was staring at me, obviously ready to get back to the race.

The dirt road ahead soon led us to another man-made culvert, though this one was altogether bigger than the previous one Gobi had jumped across. I didn't stop at all this time, just picked her up and lifted her over.

There was a moment when I had her in front of me, her face level with mine, that I swore she gave me a look of genuine love and gratitude.

"You're ready, aren't you, girl?" I said, unable to stop smiling as I put her back down and watched her start to jump about. "Let's go, then."

It was only when I looked up that I saw an old guy on a donkey. He was watching us both, his face completely expressionless.

What must I look like? I wondered.

7

RACE ORGANIZERS LIKE TO TEASE RUNNERS, and the final stretch of the day went on for miles. My GPS watch told me that we were close to finishing, but I couldn't catch a glimpse of the camp anywhere. All I could see was the path disappearing off into the distance, rising and falling over a series of ridges.

I was a couple of miles out, and by my calculations, I'd lost so much time when my pace had dropped earlier and then when I helped Gobi across the river, that Tommy and possibly even Julian would have finished. So I was surprised when I crested one of the ridges and saw both of them a mile up ahead. Neither of them appeared to be going at a decent pace. Instead, it looked to me like they were walking. I wondered whether, maybe, Tommy was holding back deliberately to allow others to catch up and make amends for what had happened earlier. Or maybe he was just struggling in the heat and was unable to go any faster.

Either way, I thought I might just have a shot at narrowing the gap between us, but I wanted to do it without letting them know. I didn't want them to realize I was chasing them down and pick up their own pace. I had only so much more energy to give for the day. As the road went down into another dip, hiding me from view, I sprinted as fast as I possibly could. When I reached the top and could be seen again, I slowed right down. Gobi thought it was all great fun and pushed me hard on the sprints.

I didn't see Tommy or Julian for the first couple of ridges, but when I crested the third, the gap between us had been halved. They were definitely walking, and I ran the next two dips even faster.

I knew I was getting closer with each sprint, and when I came up for the fifth time, my lungs burning, I was barely two hundred feet behind them. They were just about to disappear from view for the final dip down, and I could see that the finish line was just ahead.

I had time for one last sprint before I switched tactics and started to run with a bit of stealth. The last thing I wanted to do was alert them to the fact that I was chasing them, so I went from running as fast as I could to running as quietly as possible.

By keeping up on my toes, and taking care to avoid any loose stones, two hundred feet soon turned into one hundred. Then eighty. Then sixty. I was amazed that neither of them heard me or looked back.

When the gap between us was thirty feet, and the line was another hundred feet beyond them, I decided I was close enough and kicked into the fastest sprint I could manage. I got a few paces closer before Julian turned and saw me, but even though Tommy started running, I had gained too much ground for either of them to make up.

I crossed the line first, with Gobi close on my heels in second. The sound of the finishing drum couldn't drown out the shouts and cheers from the small crowd of organizers and volunteers.

I knew that the few seconds I'd put on Tommy would make no difference at all when it came to the end of the seven-day race, but it felt like a good way to respond to what had happened. I wanted him to know that even though I respected him and all he'd achieved as a runner, I wasn't going to sit back and let him have everything his own way. If he was going to win, he'd have to do battle with me out on the course fair and square.

"That was amazing," said one of the race organizers. "You're having a super race."

"Oh, thanks," I said. But I didn't want to have my ego stroked. I wanted to see how she was going to deal with the Tommy situation. "Can I come and have a chat with you later today about Tommy Chen cutting the course before checkpoint one? I'm not in the right frame of mind now, but you need to know what happened earlier."

A lot of the anger had gone, but I knew I still had to be careful about what I said. After all, Tommy was the star of the show.

I ended up giving my version of events and waiting in the tent with Gobi curled up at my side while the investigation continued. The woman asking the questions also spoke with the other runners, the checkpoint staff, and Tommy. I'd said that I thought a fifteen-minute adjustment was fair, but in the end Tommy had just five minutes added onto his day's time.

I was a bit disappointed and maybe a bit worried about how Tommy would take it. I went in search of him and found him in his tent. He was in tears.

"Do you have a minute to talk, Tommy?"

"I didn't see the markers," he said as soon as we got outside. I thought that was unlikely. Those little pink squares were hard to miss, and any seasoned runner who spends time at the front of the pack quickly learns how important it is to continually scan the route ahead and keep on course. Besides, he was behind me at the time, and my bright yellow shirt was hard to miss.

"Okay," I said. "I don't want any hard feelings about today. It's all done with now. Let's not hold any grudges, shall we?"

He looked at me, his face set firm and his tears long gone. "I didn't mean to do it. I didn't spot the markers."

I left it at that. There was nothing else to say.

Back in my tent I got a bit of encouragement from Richard and Mike for finishing first, but it was the incident with Tommy that they wanted to talk about. I wasn't so interested in discussing it and wanted to put the whole thing behind me.

"I take my hat off to you, Dion," said Richard. "You did something nice there."

"How come?"

"Us runners farther back really appreciate your taking a stand on this. We've all got to stick to the same rules. Plus, you've done the right thing talking to Tommy and burying the hatchet."

"Yeah, well, we'll see what Tommy's capable of tomorrow," I said. "Maybe I've just stirred up a whole hornets' nest of trouble for myself."

I didn't get much sleep again that night. It was hot in the tent, and I had too much white noise playing out in my head. At one point Richard left to go to the bathroom, and when he came back, Gobi growled at him. I liked the feeling that she was looking out for me.

The next day was a desert session over rocky, hard-packed ground under a cruel sun. We'd already agreed the night before that it would be too much for Gobi, so she'd travel to the next camp in a volunteer's car. I was up early, out of my tent way before my usual fifteen-minute mark, trying to find out who was going to take her and making sure that person was going to keep her cool and hydrated throughout the day.

When it came time to say goodbye, I felt a tiny shiver of worry about her. She'd attached herself so clearly to me, but would she be okay with a bunch of strangers for the day? Would I see her again, or would she set off on another adventure?

The day's race was a hard run right from the start, partly because of the change in terrain. Where the previous day had served up a mix of undulating paths, rivers, and boulders to keep runners alert, the fourth day was a series of endless flats between checkpoints that hid beneath the horizon, miles and miles apart.

Underfoot there were the same old rocks that had snagged plenty of runners' feet already, but instead of scrubland or dusty trails, we were now running across the compressed shingle that made up the black portion of the Gobi Desert.

I spent the whole day running into a headwind, watching out for rocks, and trying not to get frustrated by the constant sound of eating and drinking that was coming from over my shoulder.

It was Tommy.

Almost from the start of the day, he had positioned himself behind me. Not ten feet behind me or a few feet to the side. Right behind me, his feet falling in perfect sync with mine. With his body tucked in where the wind resistance was at its weakest, he was slipstreaming, just like a road cyclist or a migratory bird. Only, with Tommy, it was obvious he had no intention of ever giving me a break and taking the lead for a while.

As he ran behind me, leaving me to navigate the route and suck up the vicious headwind, he got himself fuelled.

Nuts. Gels. Water.

He spent the whole day eating and drinking and saying absolutely nothing to me. Even when Zeng overtook us both, Tommy didn't move. He was my shadow, and there was nothing I could do about it.

I started to wonder about Tommy's motives. What was he up to? Did he plan on stalling me? Was he planning to break away and leave me in his dust? I knew he would want to erase yesterday's loss and be all about winning the stage, so why was he staying behind me? Then I started to think about Gobi. I missed her biting at my gaiters to get me to speed up.

For most of the day, though, I coped well enough and refused to let Tommy's presence get me down. In fact, it gave me the extra incentive I needed to ignore the headwind, put up with the boredom, and grind out a steady, solid pace.

At least, that's how I felt until we approached the final checkpoint. I knew it was just over four miles from the finish, but with the sun now at its highest in the sky and the temperature feeling like it was in the low hundreds, I started to feel dizzy.

When I was finally in the shade of the checkpoint, I took a moment to enjoy the lack of heat and steady myself. Tommy, on the other hand, didn't even pause. He nodded and exchanged a couple of words with one of the team and carried straight on. I don't think he even broke stride.

I decided to take my time, filling up both my water bottles so that I had the full fifty ounces. When I finally moved out, Tommy was six hundred feet ahead of me. He looked strong and in perfect control. It was clear he was on a mission, and I soon realized there was no way I was going to catch him.

Julian and Zeng caught me soon after and didn't waste any time behind me. They went off in a pair, hunting Tommy down, while I felt as though my wheels had just come off.

I couldn't get going. No matter how hard I tried, no matter how much I told myself not to slow down, I could feel my legs turn to concrete.

This wasn't like the day before, when the boredom and fatigue had been equal factors. This was purely physical. I'd spent three hours running in full heat into a scorching headwind. I simply didn't have much strength left.

I'd been here before.

It was back in 2013. Even though I'd got my weight down from 240 pounds to the mid-170s, I still had the taste for good food and good wine. So when it came to choosing my first-ever marathon to complete, I picked one that took place in France, in the heart of wine country. Each mile marker had a refreshment station that offered either local wine or local delicacies. And because it was all about the good vibes and not about the time, all the runners had to dress up as animals.

I went as a pig.

Some people skipped a few of the stations, but not me. By the time I reached the halfway point, I'd put away vast quantities of meat, cheese, and oysters as well as a half-dozen glasses of wine. I had a little bit of pain from where my skin was chafing at about the three-quarter mark, then developed some leg and lower back pain just after the twenty-mile point.

The sun was getting fierce, and even though Lucja was dancing about like a prizefighter at the end of a first-round knockout, I slowed down. I felt nauseated; I was finding it hard to concentrate or see straight, and the sharp, stabbing pain in my back had me seriously worried.

Lucja got me to the end that day, though I barely remember

the final mile. She helped me back to the hotel, got me drinking plenty of water, and told me that it would all be okay as I shivered beneath the blankets on the bed.

We were only a few months away from our first 155-mile multi-stage ultra—an event that would see us cross parts of the inhospitable, unforgiving Kalahari Desert in South Africa. Lucja's training had been going well, and we both knew she'd be fine. But me? Who was I kidding?

"I can't do it, Lucja. I'm just not like you."

"Just sleep on it, Dion. We'll worry about it tomorrow."

Tommy was too far ahead for me to see him, and Julian and Zeng were almost out of sight too. I was finished. There was nothing left. My legs were like strangers to me, and my head was drifting into thoughts I couldn't control.

Maybe this was going to be my last race after all.

Maybe I was all washed up.

Maybe coming here had been one big mistake.

I heard the drum long before I saw the finish line. I'd been overtaken by a fourth runner in the final mile, but I was past caring. All I wanted was for the day to be over. For everything to be over. I could imagine Lucja telling me to sleep on it, that I'd feel better after some rest and food, but another voice within was telling me to pack it all in completely.

When I turned the final bend and saw the finish line, Gobi was there. She was sitting in the shade, on a rock, scanning the horizon.

For a moment she stayed motionless, and I wondered whether she'd recognize me.

Then she was a blur of brown fur in motion. Leaping from the rock, she tore over the ground towards me, tail up, little tongue flapping.

For the first time that day, I was smiling.

It had been the hottest day yet, and the sun was dangerously intense. The camp was near an old sheep station, and I tried to rest up in one of the barns, but the metal sides had turned it into a furnace. I settled for the tent, where the air was stale and the temperature was above 110 degrees. With Gobi curled up at my side, I drifted in and out of sleep. Part of me was looking forward to the chance to lie back and recover, but these times in the tent were the moments when I missed Lucja most of all.

Even before I came to China, I knew racing was going to be hard without her there. Work commitments meant she couldn't join me, but this was only the second race we hadn't entered together. And even though we hadn't run side by side since that first marathon in France, where I'd dressed as a pig—with her as a bumblebee—I relied on her in so many ways, especially at the end of each day. She'd be the one who would get out of the tent and be sociable with the other runners, and whenever I became frustrated or was bothered by something, she'd always help take the sting out of it. In more than one race, she'd talked me out of quitting entirely. I needed her, especially when unexpected problems came up as they did with Tommy.

But today had taught me something else. I missed Gobi. She was a great distraction from the boredom of hour after hour of running across an unchanging landscape. The way she ran—determined, consistent, committed—inspired me too. She was a fighter who refused to give up. She didn't let hunger or thirst or fatigue slow her down. She just kept going.

It was a bittersweet moment, for I knew what was coming tomorrow.

Day five was the long stage. Almost fifty miles in even hotter temperatures. I'd already made arrangements for Gobi to be looked after by the organizers again, and I knew they'd take good care of her.

Long days have always been my speciality, even more so when the heat is cranked up. But after only two days of running with Gobi at my side, something had changed. I was beginning to enjoy running with her, watching her little legs power through the day. I knew I'd miss her again.

I didn't get much sleep that night. The air was too hot and still to get comfortable, and after four days of running without having a shower or even changing my clothes, my skin was coated in a thick layer of dried sweat and dirt. Gobi couldn't settle either. She got up a few times, trotting out of the tent to go and bark at the sheep. I didn't mind, and nobody else in the tent complained. I guess we were all too busy trying to get our heads ready for what was coming next.

8

I MIGHT HAVE GROWN UP IN AUSTRALIA, BUT I still have to train for the heat. Living in Edinburgh means going months without the temperature rising above 60 degrees, and if I didn't take matters into my own hands, I'd not be able to cope out in the desert.

The solution was to turn the spare bedroom at home into a mini heat chamber. I bought two industrial heaters—the kind you'd expect to see drying out a house that's been flooded—as well as two small portables. I bought a heavy blind for the window and discovered that if it's just me in there, the thermometer will top out at 100 degrees. If I can persuade Lucja to join me, it'll rise a little higher.

The sessions are brutal. I wear winter running tights, a hat, and gloves, and set the incline on the treadmill as high as it will go. The humidity is intense, and even when I don't wear a backpack loaded with six or seven kilos (thirteen to fifteen pounds) of sugar or rice, I still struggle as I get into the second and third hour.

I'd put in more of these sessions in my training for the Gobi Desert event than I had for any other race. And when I wanted to change things up and run in some scorching dry heat, I'd pay a hundred pounds for an hour-long session in the heat chamber at the local university. Lucja said she'd never seen me so determined and focused, and I knew I had no other option. I'd run the Marathon des Sables twice already, where the heat even topped 130 degrees from time to time, but I'd never felt much pressure to perform back then. At Gobi, I knew it would be different. The guys on the podium would be the ones who coped with the heat.

Day five started an hour earlier, at seven o'clock, and as I stood on the start line, I went through my race plan for the hundredth time. Go quick through the road section at the start, take the desert section steady but strong, and then—depending on the heat—drop the hammer and race it home. I was still third overall, but there were just twenty minutes separating number one from number four. I needed a good day. I simply could not afford to mess up anything.

From the beginning of the day, I ran the way I wanted. I was out front, leading the pack at times and then dropping back to let someone else carry the burden for a while. I was concentrating hard on my stride and missed the markers at one point. I led the pack the wrong way for a minute until someone called us back. We tracked back, still in formation, to where the runner was waiting for us to resume the lead. There was no need for anyone to try and get an unfair advantage. The course and the heat were enough of a challenge by themselves.

The terrain was less helpful. The first six miles were through thick tufts of camel grass occasionally interrupted by brief sections of uneven asphalt. After that, we moved onto the "Black Gobi" sand. It was still early, but already it felt like the temperature was more than a hundred. It was obvious that the heat was going to be cruel, and I let myself ease up a little on the pace. A couple of people overtook me, but I didn't mind. I had a plan to stick to and guessed that in a few hours, as the sun really started to attack, I'd be overtaking anyone who had pushed himself too hard in this middle section.

I let my mind drift to Gobi, wondering what she was doing while I was running. I also made a point of noticing the scenery around us, knowing that I was unlikely to see it ever again, and hoping to keep my mind from slipping into boredom. As soon as we had hit the black sand, all signs of human life fell away. On previous days we had run through remote villages where curious locals stood and watched in the shade of their single-storey houses. At other times the route had taken us along dried-up riverbeds as wide as a football field where people stopped and stared, and across wide-open plains where the ground was the colour of fire. But as we pushed deeper into the Gobi Desert, there were no signs of human life. Nobody could make a life for himself in terrain so brutal.

As I entered the fourth checkpoint, I went through my usual routine of filling my bottles, taking a salt tablet, and asking about the temperature.

"It's 115 degrees now," the medic said. "But it's going to hit 120 soon enough. You want one of these?" He handed me a hot Pepsi. It was the only time the organizers had given us anything other than water to drink. Even though I could almost feel it burn my throat, I gulped it straight down.

"Thanks," I said. "You got any rehydrate solution?" I'd been popping salt tablets throughout the day, but with half the race still to come, I wanted to make sure I had enough to last. He took one of my bottles and made up a salt and sugar drink.

"You sure you're okay?" he said, taking a closer look at me as he handed it back.

"I'm fine. I'm just taking precautions."

Before I left, I checked the timings of the runners ahead of me. Tommy, Zeng, and Julian were among them, and they were only a quarter of an hour up the road. I was surprised they weren't further ahead and decided to step up the pace a bit. After all, I was hydrated, I'd just taken on an extra 150 calories from the Pepsi, and it was getting hot. I was ready to attack and knew that if I stayed strong, I'd probably catch them within the next one or two checkpoints.

I caught Julian at the next one, checkpoint five. He didn't look great, but he didn't look finished either. What interested me was the fact that Tommy and Zeng had left only minutes before I'd arrived. I quickly dug in my bag and pulled out the secret weapon I'd been holding in reserve this whole race. My tiny iPod.

I clipped it on, poked the earbuds in, and hit play as I headed back out into the heat. I knew the thing only had a few hours of battery life, which is why I'd never turned it on during any of the long afternoons I'd spent in the tent or at any other point in the race. I'd wanted to keep it for a moment when I needed a boost, and this was the perfect opportunity.

I listened to the playlist I had carefully put together over the previous months. The list included some big songs, a few surging anthems that I knew would get my feet going. But the real rocket fuel was Johnny Cash. When that baritone filled my ears with lyrics about outsiders and the kind of men everyone always writes off, I felt my spirit lift. He was singing just to me, calling me to push harder, run faster, and prove the doubters wrong.

When I finally saw Tommy at checkpoint seven, he looked awful. He was slumped on a chair, and two or three volunteers were desperately trying to cool him down, spraying him with water and fanning him with their clipboards. He looked at me, and I could tell right then that I had him.

I turned away to give him some privacy, filled my bottles, and popped another salt tablet. Zeng had just left the checkpoint, and in front of him was a guy we all called Brett, a Kiwi runner who was having an excellent day, and an American female runner named Jax. I knew I could still win the stage, but I also knew I didn't need to. I wasn't concerned about Brett and Jax's finishing ahead of me because both their overall times were hours behind mine.

All that mattered was that I passed Zeng, who was probably now five minutes ahead of me for the stage; as long as I did that, the twenty-minute overall lead I held on him before the day started would remain. With only six miles to race in the last day stage, there was no way I could lose the overall time, and the winner's medal would be mine. There were two checkpoints left to run, and a total of ten or twelve miles. If I kept going like I had been, I'd do it.

As I was putting some water on my head, I listened to what the doctor was saying to Tommy.

"You're very hot, Tommy, and we'd rather you go out with Dion than on your own. Will you do that?"

I fiddled with my earbuds and pretended not to hear. I didn't want to leave the guy stranded, but I was racing to win. If he couldn't keep up, I wasn't going to carry him.

As I checked my bag straps and prepared to move off, Tommy pushed himself off the seat and stood next to me.

"Are you sure you're okay, Tommy?"

"Yeah," he said, his voice hoarse and faint. "I'm just struggling. It's too hot."

We moved out. In the few minutes that I'd been in the shade

of the checkpoint, someone had turned up the heat a few more degrees. It was like running in a forced-air oven, and the sun cut like needles into the flesh on my arms. I was loving it. Even though I wondered whether I should have reapplied the sunscreen I'd put on in the morning, nothing could wipe the smile from my face.

There was no breeze and no shade. Everything was hot—the air, the rocks, even the plastic trim and metal zippers on my backpack. All that existed out there was heat.

But I knew I wanted to catch Zeng. I didn't know how strong he was or whether he was struggling, but I knew I felt about as good as I possibly could, given the conditions. This was my chance. I had to take it.

We were only a few hundred feet out from the checkpoint, and already Tommy was struggling to keep up. But he was a tough runner, and he wasn't going to give up on the race anytime soon.

We were in a straight gravel section, one where the pink markers were placed every fifty feet. "Come on, Tommy," I said, trying to get him to pick up his pace. "Let's run the flags."

We ran to the first marker, then walked to the next one before running again. We carried on like that for a half mile, and soon the track became sandy and opened out into an even wider area. All around us were sand canyons, twenty-foot-high walls of compressed dust and dirt as far as the eye could see. It looked like the surface of Mars, and if it was possible, I could have sworn that there was even less air and more heat in there.

Tommy was no longer at my side. I knew he'd drop back eventually. *This is it*, I thought. *Time to move.*

I ran through four or five flags, feeling my breathing hold steady and my pace remain solid. It felt good to be running free again, good to know that with every step I was reeling in the guy ahead.

And yet there was something nagging me. I couldn't stop thinking about Tommy. Was he okay? Was he still with me? Was he going to make it out here on his own?

I slowed down.

I stopped.

And then I looked back.

Tommy was swaying like a drunkard. His arms were flailing, his balance destroyed. He looked as though he was in an earthquake, and each step forward was a battle against invisible forces. I watched him, willing him to shake it off and start running toward me.

Come on, Tommy. Don't bail on me now.

It was a futile wish, and within a few seconds I was running the three hundred feet back to where he was swaying and staggering on the spot.

"Tommy, tell me what's going on."

"Too hot." His words were slurred, and I had to grab him to stop him from falling over. It was a little after one in the afternoon, and the sun was directly above us. I knew it was only going to get hotter, and I looked about for some shade, but there was none at all, just a series of windblown rocks off to the side.

I checked my watch. We were just over a mile into the section with another three to go until the next checkpoint. I thought about telling him to turn back, but he was in no state to go anywhere by himself. It was all up to me.

Do I go back, or do I go on? I wondered.

Tommy fumbled for his water bottles. One was completely empty, and he drained the other in a couple of gulps. I guessed that we'd left the checkpoint twenty or thirty minutes before, and that when we did, Tommy must have left with full bottles. That meant he'd drunk seventy ounces in no time at all.

"I need to pee," he said, pulling down his pants. His urine was like molasses.

He slumped down in the sand, right in the full glare of the sun. "Need to sit," he said. "I need to sit. Can you wait?"

"There's no sitting here, Tommy. You've got to get into some shade." I looked back to see if I'd missed anything, but there was nothing that could shield him from the sun. I hoped I'd see some other runners too, but there was nobody.

I scanned ahead. I thought I could see a path of shade to the side of a rock formation about a mile in the distance. It looked as though it might be big enough to offer Tommy some protection from the sun, and it struck me as our best hope.

It took another twenty minutes to reach it. I had to drag Tommy with one arm through the sand while carrying his backpack and giving him as much of my water as he wanted. I tried to keep him talking, but I couldn't think of much more to say than "Keep coming, mate. We're nearly there." He barely said a single word in return.

I knew how serious Tommy's condition was. He was dizzy, disoriented, and soaked in sweat. It was a clear case of heat exhaustion, and I knew that if I didn't cool him down soon, it could slip into heatstroke. From that point he'd be at risk of falling into a coma in as few as thirty minutes. After that he would need special medical equipment to keep him alive.

I finally managed to drag him to the sand rock and put him in the small rectangle of shade that fell beside it. I unzipped his shirt, hoping to let out any heat that I could. I was shocked by how pale his skin was. He looked half-dead already.

Tommy half fell onto his side and peed some more. His urine was even darker this time.

What am I going to do? I could feel the urge to panic but fought as hard as I could to keep my emotions in check. I guessed that we were probably halfway through the stage. I ran up a slight hill to see if there were any signs of life, but there was nothing and no one around.

"Listen, Tommy," I said as I crouched back at his side. "You need help. I'm going to keep going to the next checkpoint and get them to drive back to you, okay?"

"I don't want to run anymore," he said.

"I know, mate. You don't have to. Just stay here and wait for them to come. Don't move."

I gave him the last of my water, made sure his feet were tucked up in the shade, and ran.

My head was full of numbers. I calculated I had just lost forty-five minutes. I had given away the last forty ounces of my water, and I had just under three miles left to run before I could get any more. It was 120 degrees and likely to get even hotter over the next hour. If I hadn't looked back when I did, Tommy might already have spent thirty minutes in heatstroke. If I hadn't looked back, he might have already slipped into a coma.

As I ran, I scanned ahead for the markers but also looked far into the distance in the hope of seeing a vehicle or someone else who could help. Still nothing.

After the numbers came the questions. Why had I looked back in the first place? Had I sensed something? Was something or someone guiding me to help Tommy? And had I made the right decision to run ahead? Would Tommy have got help quicker if I'd gone back?

To save time, I tried to cut the course. I lost the markers for a while and started to panic. I was in a gully, feeling trapped. My heart was racing, and I feared, for the first time, that I might have made a terrible mistake.

I cleared a ridge and saw that I was back on track. In the distance, a mile off, I could see the checkpoint. It shimmered like a mirage, and no matter how fast I tried to run, it didn't appear to get any closer.

Half a mile out, a race vehicle approached. I waved it down and told them about Tommy and where to find him.

"You've got to get there quickly," I said. "He's in real trouble. And I'm out of water myself. You haven't got any water, have you?"

The little they had was enough to get me to the checkpoint, and as soon as I made it there, I sat down and ran through the Tommy story again. I took on as much water as I could and ran through my symptoms. But having run with too little water in me and too much pressure to raise the alarm, I'd already pushed myself too hard. I was feeling queasy and weak. At least I was aware of my symptoms. That meant I was thinking straight. I didn't have heat exhaustion, yet.

I asked about Zeng and was surprised to hear that he was only twenty minutes ahead. Twenty minutes? That meant the overall result was in the balance. Zeng had cancelled out the lead I'd had on him at the start of the day, but I still had a chance.

I found it hard not to think about death as I ran. I wondered if we were near the place where the other runner had died of heat-stroke back in 2010. And I thought about Tommy too. I felt sad to think that he might be in a coma even now. I hoped he wasn't. I hoped I'd done enough. Suddenly, having been so angry about him gaining five minutes on us at the boulder section seemed silly.

Half a mile after leaving the checkpoint, my chest started to feel strange. It was as if it wasn't pumping correctly, as though I had a band wrapped tight around my lungs. Whenever I took a drink of water, it felt like it was boiling. Gradually I slowed down. I was feeling ill. Soon I was shuffling along, my feet scuffing and stumbling like I was half-asleep.

I was terrified of just one physical symptom: heart palpitations. I'd had them two or three times before. My chest would feel like I was going to explode, the sweat would pour out of me, and I'd feel sick and faint. The doctors had linked it to my drinking too much coffee, and ever since then I'd cut out caffeine in the build-up to a race. But the memory of it still bothered me, and out there in the heat of the Gobi Desert, I could feel the symptoms all lining up. And if my heart did start to freak out again, I knew I couldn't blame it on coffee this time. If I started having palpitations out here, it could only mean that something serious was happening.

I spotted a race vehicle parked up ahead of me. I knew it was there to offer emergency assistance, and I must have looked like a viable candidate as I staggered up. When I was close enough to hear the engine running, the volunteers jumped out.

"Are you okay? Do you want some water?"

"I need to sit in the car," I said. "I don't feel well."

I didn't know if it was in the rules or not, but I didn't care. I needed to cool down immediately.

I yanked on the rear door and threw myself and my bag down onto the backseat. The AC was on full blast, and it was like stepping into a refrigerator. It was beautiful. I closed my eyes and let the cool air get to work.

When I opened them again, I had to blink and rub my eyes to check that I had read the dash properly. "Does that really say 132 degrees?" I said.

"Yeah," said the guy behind the wheel. He and the other

volunteer didn't say anything else, but I could see him watching me closely in the rear-view mirror.

"Can I have the water?" I asked, pointing at a bottle that had a frozen cylinder of ice inside. I was convinced that it was the best drink I'd ever had in my entire life.

I pulled a gel from the pouch around my front. It was hard to get my hands to work properly, and some of the sticky substance ended up on my chin, chest, and the car seats. I figured I'd wait the ten minutes it usually takes for a gel to kick in, then be off. But as the time passed, I felt steadily worse.

My head was drifting, and I was finding it almost impossible to keep my eyes fixed on any one thing for more than a few seconds. The band around my chest wound tighter with each breath, and I could feel my lungs grow heavy within me.

"Come on," I said to myself, long after the gel should have worked. I was trying to summon the energy to pick up my bag and move, trying to command myself to get out and keep going, but nothing happened.

The cold air wasn't working as I hoped it would, but the thought of opening the door and stepping back out into that heat once more made me scared. Even if I could get my body to obey me and haul myself out of the car, could I even make it to the next checkpoint, let alone the finish?

It was at that point when my chest exploded. My heart started racing, and I was panting, desperate to pull in any air I could.

I glanced up and caught the driver looking back at me in the mirror. In his eyes I saw fear. Fear and panic.

It set off a second explosion within me. Only this time it wasn't my heart that started racing; it was my mind. For the first time ever in my life, I was genuinely scared for my safety. For the first time ever, I wondered if I was about to die.

9

COME ON! NOW, DION, NOW!

It was no use. No matter how tightly I closed my eyes or gritted my teeth, I couldn't make myself move from the back of the car. All I could do was breathe in the cold air and hope that something would change.

Minutes slipped by. I tried another gel. I tried stretching to relieve the pressure in my chest. I tried to remember my race plan. Nothing worked.

I wondered what had happened to Tommy. I hoped the car had reached him in time and the volunteers had been able to get him the help he needed. My best guess was that his race was over.

I had been looking out of the car for a few minutes when it hit me that I'd not seen any other runners for a long, long time. I thought about the gap I needed to make up.

"How did Zeng look when he came past?"

"Not great. He was struggling a lot and just walking."

That was all I needed to hear. I'd wasted fifteen minutes in the car, so I now needed to make up thirty-five. If he was still having a hard time, there was a chance I could do it. And if I did, I'd be in the overall lead.

I got out of the car with some trepidation but anxious to make up for the time I'd lost. I could feel the heat, and it took me a while to catch my breath and steady my feet. But eventually I was running again. Not fast, but steady.

That pace didn't last very long. I had enough energy to run only a few hundred feet, but after that I was walking again. At least my heart had stopped its wild beating, and I was able to think more clearly. I managed to run the flags for the remaining miles, stumbling ahead, looking at nothing but the pink markers before me, and thinking about nothing other than placing one foot in front of the other.

Eventually I was confronted by a series of tall, wind-formed cliffs. I crested a sand dune that ran through the middle and saw the finish line up ahead.

Just like the day before, Gobi was waiting for me in the shade. She ran out to join me for the last two hundred feet, but as soon as we crossed the line, she ran, panting, back to the shade, where she collapsed in a heap.

"Any news on Tommy?" I asked one of the volunteers.

He smiled and arched his eyebrows. "It's amazing," he said. "They got him cooled down, and eventually he started walking again. Filippo's with him, and they're doing okay."

I knew Filippo Rossi, a Swiss runner who was having a good day. I was delighted and relieved in equal measure to hear that he and Tommy were together.

The two other finishers—Brett and Zeng—had clearly been home for a while, and when I saw that the gap between Zeng and me was forty minutes, I knew he'd nailed it. We had the one stage left to run, and since it was only a handful of miles, I would never be able to make up that time in so short a distance.

When Tommy finally crossed the line with Filippo at his side, the whole camp was buzzing. Everyone knew what had happened by then, and Tommy's remarkable recovery and resilience were given all the praise they deserved. Nobody seemed to know anything about my helping him in the first place, but I didn't mind so much. What meant more was the hug Tommy gave me when he first saw me. He was in tears, and I was welling up. There was no need to say anything at all.

I waited in my tent as I had done every afternoon, drifting in and out of sleep with Gobi curled up at my side. I hoped none of the other runners still out on the course had come as close as Tommy had to being in serious trouble, and I wondered how Richard, Mike, Allen, and the Macau boys were. Despite the less-than-perfect start, I'd come to like the Macau boys. They genuinely cared for one another and had spent every evening giving one another massages. They were good guys, and, in a way, I was going to miss them.

It struck me that I could have won the race but only if I hadn't stopped to help Tommy. That didn't seem like a price worth paying, just to finish one place higher on the podium, even if it would have been my first overall multi-stage victory and a huge boost for my running future. Stopping to help Tommy had cost me, but I was glad with the way things worked out. Assuming that everything went okay on the final six-mile stage of the last day, my second-place podium position was secure. I wasn't ready to celebrate, but I was happy enough. I had already proved to myself that my running career still had some life left in it.

Darkness had fallen by the time Richard, Mike, and Allen got back. They'd been out in the sun all day, and they were suffering for it. They looked like the walking dead, stumbling around the tent, their faces equal parts red with sunburn and pale with exhaustion. But it was over, and by the time the last one was back, the mood in the tent was different. Everyone relaxed more than usual, relieved to be so near the end of the race.

I woke up to the sound of the tent falling down. There was no sign of the Macau boys, and Mike was shouting at us to get up. I scooped up Gobi and crawled outside. A wind had struck up from nowhere, bringing the sand with it. It stung, but Gobi and I joined the others and lay on top of the tent to prevent it from flying off while Richard went in search of help.

The night was full of the sounds of two-way radios crackling, tents being flattened, and Chinese voices shouting back and forth. By the light of dozens of headlamps, I could see the volunteers running around the camp, desperately trying to put the tents back up.

The wind picked up and developed into a full-on sandstorm. It was impossible to see anything that was more than two or three hundred feet away, and we heard that the last runners out on the course had been held at checkpoints and were being driven back to camp.

After an hour of waiting for someone to come and help with the tent, I called Gobi to follow and went in search of a woman called Nurali. She had been introduced to us when we arrived at the first camp site. I'd been watching her shout orders and grow increasingly frustrated with her team as the winds raged.

"Can you get your guys to put up our tent, please?" I said to her.

"Yes, but we have many tents to put up first."

"I know you do," I said, "but we asked an hour ago, and still nothing's happened."

"Not my problem," she shouted.

I knew she was under a lot of pressure, and I could sympathize with her doing battle with the elements, but this seemed a little dismissive to me. "No," I said, "we've all paid thirty-seven hundred dollars to be here. It is your problem."

She muttered something I couldn't understand, turned, and walked off.

The wind picked up, and a sense of panic rose among the people running around. It was the kind of wind we get up in the highlands of Scotland, so maybe that's why I wasn't so worried. The sand didn't bother me either. All I had to do was copy what Gobi did and curl up tight with my head away from the wind, and I found I was fine.

After midnight we heard that the sandstorm was about to get worse. Nobody was getting any sleep, and after fifty miles of exhausting running, we all needed to recover, so the organizers decided to abandon the camp for the night. We joined the other runners who were huddled against one of the many large rock formations and waited for the buses to come. The level of fear in the air seemed to increase as we stood there, and before long the dust and sand were in our mouths, ears, and eyes. But I knew it was just another uncomfortable set of feelings to get through. We'd all experienced far worse in the previous twenty-four hours, but the unknown is always more intimidating than the familiar.

As dawn broke, the bus took us to a low building at the entrance to a national park twenty minutes away. It was a strange little museum with displays of million-year-old fossils and dioramas that showed a wide and random collection of natural habitats. Of course, Gobi made herself at home, especially in the rainforest section that was full of fake trees and fake plants. I couldn't help laughing when she relieved herself under one of them.

Within minutes we had trashed the whole place, turning it into a refugee camp for 101 sweaty, smelly runners—and one not-quite-house-trained dog. The museum staff didn't mind, for the shop at the other end of the museum was selling drinks and snacks at a record rate.

The day was already scheduled as a rest day, given the gruelling nature of the previous long stage, and we spent the time sleeping, eating snacks, drinking sodas, and talking among ourselves.

I didn't retreat into my sleeping bag or take off somewhere else. Instead, I stayed and talked with Richard, Mike, and Allen.

"What are you going to do about that little one?" said Mike in the afternoon, pointing at Gobi.

It was a good question, and one that I'd been asking myself during the long stage. I knew that the two days I'd run without Gobi had been hard and that somehow I'd got attached to her. I didn't want to leave her to fend for herself out here.

There was more to it than that. Gobi had chosen me. I didn't know why, but I knew it was true. She had a hundred other runners to choose from, and dozens of volunteers and staff, but from the very first time I saw her and she started nibbling at my gaiters, she had hardly ever chosen to leave my side.

Gobi was a tough little trouper too. She had run more than seventy miles over three legs of the race without eating a thing during the day, and I'm sure that given the chance, she would have clocked up a whole lot more. She obviously had been scared of water but had pushed ahead and trusted me to help her. She had given everything she had to keep up with me. How could I leave her behind when I finished the race?

For every reason I could find for wanting to help Gobi, there were equally strong arguments for walking away. I had no idea what kinds of diseases she was carrying, whether she belonged to anyone, or how I could even go about doing something to help. This was China, after all. I was pretty sure that not a lot of people would be queuing up if I asked for volunteers to help me find a home for a stray dog of unknown origin. If the stories were true, wasn't there a chance she'd end up getting killed and eaten by someone?

So I didn't do anything about finding her a forever home right there in China. I didn't ask any of the many race crew members who had taken a shine to Gobi, and I didn't even bring it up with my tent mates.

I didn't ask because it wasn't an option I wanted to consider.

I had a better plan.

"You know what, Mike? I've made up my mind. I'm going to find a way to bring her home with me."

It was the first time I'd spoken those words out loud, but as soon as I said them, I knew it was the right thing to do. I had no idea if it was even possible, but I knew I had to try.

"That's great," said Mike. "I'll chuck in a few quid to help out if you like."

"Really?"

"Me too," said Richard.

I was amazed and touched as well. As far as I could tell, all Gobi had done for my tent mates was growl when they came back in the tent at night, keep them awake by chasing sheep, and beg them for scraps of food anytime she caught them eating. But I was wrong. In the same way Gobi had inspired me, she'd inspired them a bit too.

"Any dog that tough," said Richard, "deserves a happy ending."

By the time we lined up on the start for the final day, the sandstorm had passed. As in all multi-stage ultras, the final day is nearly always a short run of between six and ten miles. And, like in every other multi-stage I'd been in before, the thought of being an hour or two away from the final finish line brought out the best in the runners. While they'd been hobbling around like the walking dead during the recovery day in the museum, they set off at the start of the last day as if it were a Saturday morning sprint down at the park.

I had Gobi by my side, and she seemed to know something special was going on. She didn't chew my gaiters as we ran. Instead, she kept perfect pace with me, occasionally looking up at me with her big dark eyes.

The weather was cool with a slight drizzle as we ran, and I was happy that Gobi wouldn't overheat. There were no checkpoints because the last stage was so short, so I stopped every couple of miles to give her some water from my hand. She never refused, and it amazed me how much she had learned to trust me in just a few days.

I'd spent a bit of time looking at the race positions while we were in the museum. As I'd suspected, I had no chance of catching Zeng, and Tommy's near escape had cost him dearly. He'd been overtaken by Brett, the Kiwi who had stormed to victory on the long stage. I was still twenty minutes ahead of Brett, and if I kept ahead of Brett, my second-place finish would be secure.

I'd done just that all the way, but as I stopped at the halfway stage on the crest of a sandy hill to give Gobi a drink, I saw Brett approach me from behind. He stopped next to me. I must have given him a quizzical look, for he smiled and shrugged.

"I could hardly run past you as you're giving her a drink, could I?"

I smiled back. "Thanks," I said.

I put the bottle back in its holder on my bag's shoulder strap, gave Brett a nod, and carried on racing as though nothing had happened.

We stayed like that for the rest of the stage. I finished the stage fifth, Brett sixth, with Gobi between us. Medals were given out and photos taken straightaway, and soon afterward a celebration feast ensued with beer and a traditional barbecue, kebabs, and breads as big as pizzas stuffed with herbs and meat and all kinds of delicious things. I savoured mouthfuls of delicious mutton and let Gobi lick the grease from my fingers. There was a lot of laughing and hugging and the kind of smiles you get only when you know you're surrounded by good people, enjoying a moment that you're going to remember for years to come.

I had started the race as I always did, keeping to myself, focusing on the run and nothing else. I ended it as I have ended every other race, surrounded by friends.

But the race across the Gobi Desert was different. The lows had been lower, and the highs had been higher. The experience had changed my life. So it was only right that in return I should do everything I could to help change Gobi's.

PART 3

10

I WATCHED GOBI FROM OUT OF THE BUS WIN-dow. She was busy eating up all the scraps of kebab that had been left behind from the barbecue. Nurali was organizing the rest of the volunteers who had just loaded the last of the runners onto the other bus. Gobi stopped. She looked up. Was it just me, or had she worked out that something was wrong? The bus engine kicked into life. Gobi, startled a little, started running up and down. She looked just like she did when I turned back at the river. She was looking for something. For someone. For me. Her tail was down, and her ears pinned back. I felt an almost irresistible urge to haul my aching body out of the seat, climb down out of the bus, and go and scoop her up into my arms again.

This is ridiculous, I thought to myself. I felt like a dad watching his kid walk through the gates for his first day of school.

The bus began to pull away as I watched Nurali call Gobi to her side, give her a bit of meat, and ruffle the shaggy brown mop of fur that sat like a bird's nest on the top of her head.

I sat back and tried to think of something else. Anything.

The bus journey back to Hami could not have been more different from the drive we had made away from it a week earlier. Back then I'd sat and only said a few words to my neighbour. I'd grown increasingly frustrated with the noise of the Macau boys behind me, and more than once I'd turned around hoping they'd get the hint and shut up.

On the drive to Hami, I would have paid good money to sit near the Macau boys and hear them laughing and chatting. I would have welcomed the distraction. Sadly, the three of them were on a different bus, and in the quiet that fell upon my fellow passengers as they gave in to the post-race, post-barbecue, post-beer drowsiness, I was left alone with my thoughts.

Why was this so hard? I had no idea I was going to feel this way. And this wasn't goodbye. I was going to see Gobi again in a couple of hours.

That plan was about as simple as any plan could be. Nurali, the woman who'd been kind of dismissive during the sandstorm, was going to drive Gobi back to Hami, where we'd have the award dinner, and I'd be able to say a proper goodbye to the dog. After that Nurali would take Gobi back home with her to Urumqi as I flew back to Edinburgh. I was then going to make all the arrangements to have Gobi flown back to begin her new life with Lucja, me, and Lara the cat back in the UK.

How long would it take? I didn't know.

How much would it cost? No idea.

Would Nurali look after her? Absolutely. That was one thing of which I was confident. Nurali might have been a little off with me when the camp was blowing apart, but I'd seen the way she ordered people around and got things done. She was a fixer, and I could tell that without her the whole Gobi race never would have happened. She was exactly the kind of person I was going to need to get things done. Besides, I'd seen her slip Gobi enough food treats over the week to know that Nurali had a soft spot for the dog. Gobi would be fine with her. I was sure of it—just like I was sure that I was bringing Gobi home, even if it cost me a thousand pounds and took a month or two.

Gather together a bunch of runners who haven't showered, washed, or changed their clothes for a week as they've sweated their way across a desert, and they'll smell bad. Put them all on a hot bus for two hours, and the air inside will turn about as foul and putrid as you can possibly imagine.

So as soon as we arrived back in Hami, I was desperate for a shower. I cleaned myself up and rested a little, guessing that I'd catch up with Nurali and Gobi at the meal in the evening.

By the time I arrived at the restaurant, I was kind of missing Gobi already, even though it had been only a few hours. Besides, I'd only ever seen her out in the open or in a tent. How would she cope being in a town, with roads and traffic, restaurants and hotels?

I realized that there was so much I didn't know about her. Where had she been living before she joined the race? Had she ever even been inside a house before? How would she react to being shut inside from time to time? How old was she? Perhaps most important of all, did she like cats?

So much had happened the week of the race, but months, maybe even years, of Gobi's life before the race would forever be a mystery to me. I'd watched her playing when she thought I wasn't looking, and I was pretty sure that she was less than a year or two old. As for what had happened to her beforehand, I was at a total loss. If she had been mistreated, she didn't have any scars and certainly wasn't carrying any injuries that had stopped her from running well over seventy-seven miles in total. So why had she run away? Had she got lost? Was there an owner somewhere out near the sand dune on the edge of the Gobi Desert currently fretting about his little dog who had gone missing?

Everyone I had spoken to thought this was unlikely. Gobi wasn't the only dog I'd seen on the run, and even the few hours I'd spent in Urumqi and Hami told me there must have been thousands of dogs roaming the streets in both places. Stray dogs were everywhere, and all the Chinese I had spoken to told me that Gobi must have been one of them.

At the restaurant I looked for Nurali and Gobi, but there was no sign of either of them. None of her team was there either, only the race organizers. I found one of them and asked about Nurali.

"I thought she was supposed to be coming here and bringing Gobi with her," I said.

She looked confused. "No, Nurali was never going to be coming here. She's got too much to do back at the finish line."

"Is she coming here at all before we leave tomorrow?"

"I can't think why she would."

I walked away, deflated.

It bothered me that I wasn't going to get to see Gobi to say goodbye properly. And it bothered me that the plan we'd sketched out wasn't being followed. Had something been lost in translation? Had something gone wrong already? Was Gobi still okay?

The thing that bothered me most was the fact that I could feel myself starting to stress about it. Part of me wanted to do what I normally did after a race and switch off from everything for a few weeks—from dieting, from running, from having to force myself to become so laser-focused on the one goal ahead of me. I wanted to relax and not care.

But that wasn't even an option. I did care. Feeling protective of Gobi wasn't a switch I could simply flick off.

I was distracted throughout much of the awards night, but I listened hard as Brett got up to receive his third-place medal and gave a powerful but brief speech. "What I'd like to say is that for everyone who has sacrificed their race to help other people, I take my hat off to you. It shows what great human beings are in this world."

I couldn't have put it better myself. I'd been able to do something to help Tommy, but I was far from the only one. Filippo had stopped too, and there had been so many other examples of people's putting themselves second and choosing to put someone else first. From the way the Macau boys looked out for one another to the ways people who had been total strangers at the start of the week gave constant encouragement to one another. One of the things I love most about these events is that as you push yourself to the absolute limits of physical endurance, you make some of the deepest friendships of your life.

Of course, I didn't know any of that when I signed up for my first multi-stage ultra. In fact, I wasn't even sure I'd make it to the start line, let alone finish the whole thing.

Our ultra-marathon journey began around Christmas 2012. Lucja's birthday is on 23 December, and in the months beforehand she'd been talking about wanting to move up from marathons and take on something tougher. So I'd bought her a beautiful coffee-table book called *The World's Toughest Endurance Challenges*. I'd looked through it before wrapping it, astounded by events such as the Marathon des Sables, the Yukon Arctic Ultra, and the Yak

Attack in Nepal, billed as the highest (and, I guessed, the most dangerous) bike race in the world.

This was before I'd taken part in the half marathon where I ran myself into the ground to win a free meal from my friend, so I was utterly convinced that every single one of the events in the book was beyond me. Still, I thought it might be kind of fun to dream about doing one of them one day a decade or more down the road. And in the festive atmosphere, with a bottle of champagne open beside us, I was feeling pretty good about life as I watched Lucja open the book, so I said these fateful words: "Whatever page you open to, that's the one we're going to do together."

I sat back, took a drink, and watched Lucja's eyes grow wide as she saw the cover.

"Wow," she said, looking at it front and back, "this is amazing."

She closed her eyes, opened the book to a random page, and stared.

Silence. I watched her scan the page, absorbing every detail.

"Well, Dion, it looks like we're doing the Ka-la-har-ree Extreme Marathon."

"What the hell's that?" I asked.

She didn't look up but carried on, staring at the page, calling out the brutal facts: "Northwest of South Africa, near the Namibian border . . . you run 155 miles . . . six stages over seven days . . . temperature is in the 120s . . . carry your own food . . . only get water at certain times . . . and it's in the desert."

I thought hard about my response. This was her birthday after all, and I wanted the gift to be a nice thing.

"No chance."

"What?" she said, looking up at me. "I reckon it sounds pretty good."

"Listen, Lucja, there's no way we could do that. What if something happens to one of us? And what do you mean you have to carry your own food? They don't give you anything at all? How is that even possible?"

She looked back at the book, flipped a couple of pages, and then slid it over to me and pulled out her iPad. I stared at the pages, a feeling of dread starting to grow within my guts.

"There's a whole bunch of blogs from last summer's race up here on the site," Lucja said. "And there's a Facebook page . . . and a contact form."

I stopped her. "Lucja, it says it's a couple of thousand pounds each. And that's without flights."

"So?"

"So we could just have a nice holiday in the sun somewhere. Why would we want to do something stupid like running across a desert?"

Lucja looked hard at me. It was the same look she'd given me as I lay on the couch in New Zealand and she challenged me to the run. I knew that this was one of those pivotal moments in our lives.

"You said we're doing it, Dion. So we're doing it."

I backed off, figuring that saying no was only going to make her more determined. I stopped talking about it and assumed that by the time Christmas was over, she'd have forgotten all about it.

I was wrong. After Christmas, Lucja was more determined than ever, and with the race only ten months away, she felt she had to move fast. She contacted the race rep, downloaded the application form, and told me she was ready to do it.

It was my last chance to stop her, and I threw the very best reason I could think of at her.

"How are you going to go without having a shower? What about your hair? Your nails?"

"I don't care about that. I'm not bothered. The Orange River runs through one of the stages, and I can wash my hair that day."

I tried a different line of attack: "Johannesburg's got one of the highest murder rates of any city in the world. Do you really want to fly in and out of a city like that?"

"Dion, I'm doing it. Are you going to come with me?"

I thought for a while.

"We've got to work off all our Christmas fat."

She just stared.

It was New Zealand all over again. I knew I wasn't going to be able to stop her, and I didn't want to. I'd always loved Lucja's courage and her enthusiasm, and I knew my life had been so much better since I met her. I wanted to make sure she was going to be okay out there, too, even if it meant doing something as ridiculous as running across the Kalahari Desert.

"Okay," I said. "I'm in."

I hadn't spoken to Lucja since the night I stayed in Urumqi. Some runners had paid fifty pounds to be able to send e-mails and post blogs during the race, but not me. I didn't want to be distracted, and I knew Lucja would be able to check the race organizer's website for daily updates on my times and race position. So it was in Hami, after the awards dinner, that I finally got to phone her after more than a week apart.

I was actually a little nervous. I had to find a way to tell her I wanted to bring a stray Chinese dog back to live with us. We hadn't had a dog since Curtly the Saint Bernard. Both of us had taken his death badly; we had an unspoken agreement that neither of us really wanted to go through that kind of pain again.

As I prepared to dial, I ran through my speech one more time. "Isn't it great that I finished second? And something weird happened too. A little dog followed me, and I'm beginning to wonder about maybe bringing her home to live with us."

If Lucja was on my side, I knew it would happen. If she wasn't, bringing Gobi home would be a lot harder than I thought.

The phone rang, and I took a deep breath.

Even before I could say much more than hello, Lucja started talking.

"How's Gobi?"

I was stunned. "You know about Gobi?"

"Yeah! A lot of the other runners have mentioned her in their blogs, and she's even made it into a few official race updates. She's a pretty little thing, too, isn't she?"

"Yes, she is. I wanted to talk to you about something—"

"You're bringing her home? As soon as I heard about her, I knew you'd want to."

Having been away from cities and civilization for a week, the transfer from the Urumqi train station to the airport left my head spinning. I had forgotten how crowded the city was and how impossible it was to make myself understood. Even something as simple as checking in for my three-leg flight back home took three times as long as it should have. Everywhere I went there were crowds of people, and every official stared at me with thinly veiled suspicion.

I remembered why I'd vowed never to return to China.

Had meeting Gobi changed how I felt? Perhaps. The run had

matched my previous best—second place in the 2014 Kalahari Augrabies Extreme Marathon—and it had brought Gobi into my life. But I still found it hard to imagine myself coming back. Without knowing any of the language, it was just too hard to get things done.

I was approaching the gate for my flight back to Beijing when I saw all the race organizers waiting to board.

I knew the boss had taken an interest in Gobi, and I wanted to make sure she didn't forget once she got back from the race. I thanked her for getting Nurali to look after Gobi while I went back home to make the arrangements.

She handed me her business card. "It's been fantastic to see the story of you and Gobi take shape. If we can help make it happen, we will."

It was only when I got on the plane that I wondered why I hadn't asked the boss about why Nurali hadn't shown up at the awards dinner in Hami. I guessed I didn't want to appear pushy or like I was going to be an awkward person to deal with. But as the plane taxied and I drifted off, I wondered whether maybe there was something more to it than that. I was trusting Nurali to take good care of Gobi, but did I know her that well? Why hadn't she come to Hami? Was it really just an error of communication, or was it a sign that things might not go so smoothly after all?

Don't be paranoid, I told myself. *Sleep on it. These things always look better in the morning.*

11

LUCJA MET ME AT THE EDINBURGH AIRPORT with some bad news. While I'd been flying, she'd looked into the process of bringing a dog into the UK.

"It's not going to be easy," she said. "You'd have thought the hardest part of the whole thing would be getting Gobi *out* of China, but from what I can tell it's getting her *into* Britain that's going to be tough. There's more red tape than you can imagine."

In between missing Gobi and looking forward to seeing Lucja again, I'd done a fair bit of imagining. I'd imagined Gobi held in quarantine, our having to pay astronomical vet bills, and the whole thing's taking months on end.

It turned out I was pretty much correct.

She'd need to spend four months in quarantine, and that wasn't going to be cheap. But the really bad news was where she would have to serve her time.

"Heathrow," said Lucja. "That's the only option."

By Chinese or American standards, the four hundred miles that separate our home in Edinburgh from London's main airport isn't all that much. But in the UK, it's an epic journey that costs hundreds of pounds in petrol or flights, plus even more for hotels and taxis. Life in London isn't cheap, even for dogs.

The more we looked into it, the more we discovered that Lucja had been right about the costs and complexities of bringing a dog to the UK, but we'd underestimated how hard it would be to get Gobi out. In a battle for which country could wrap up the problem in the most amount of red tape, it looked like China was going to win.

Every pet-moving service we e-mailed came back with the same answer: no. Some of them didn't elaborate, but from the ones that did, we began to understand the full depth of the problem.

In order for Gobi to leave China, she would need a blood test; then she'd have to wait thirty days before being allowed to fly out of either Beijing or Shanghai. Simple enough, perhaps, but getting her on a plane out of Urumqi meant that she first had to undergo a health check by a vet, get a microchip, and have official approval from someone, somewhere, in the Chinese government. Oh, and there was one more thing: to fly from Urumqi to Beijing or Shanghai, Gobi had to be accompanied by the person who was taking her out of the country.

"Any chance of Nurali doing all that?" said Lucja.

"I couldn't get her to put up my tent in the sandstorm. There's no way she'd do all that."

"Could we get someone to drive her to Beijing?"

A few minutes on Google and the answer was clear. A thirty-five-hour, eighteen-hundred-mile drive across mountains, deserts, and who-knows-what-else wasn't much of a Plan B.

After a week of getting nothing but rejection e-mails from pet transport companies, a chink of light emerged. A woman named

Kiki e-mailed Lucja back, saying that her company, WorldCare Pet, might be able to help, but only if we could persuade Nurali to carry out some of the essential medical work. I hoped for the best and went ahead and asked.

To my surprise as well as my gratitude, Nurali e-mailed right back. Yes, she could get Gobi seen by the vet, and yes, she could make sure Gobi had all the right tests Kiki's company required. She'd even go ahead and buy a crate so that Gobi could fly in the hold.

This was the best possible outcome.

But Gobi's move wouldn't be cheap. Kiki estimated that it would cost a minimum of £5,000 for her to get Gobi back to the UK, and we'd figured out that we'd end up spending another £1,500 on quarantine and a whole lot more on travel to and from London to visit Gobi.

Bringing Gobi to our home would cost a lot of money, and we needed to think hard about whether we could do it. Part of me wanted to pay for everything ourselves, not out of pride or anything like that, but simply because bringing Gobi back was something that I—and now Lucja—wanted to do for Gobi's sake as well as our own. We weren't bringing Gobi back as an act of charity or a show of great kindness. We were bringing her back because, strange as it might sound, she was already a part of the family. And when it comes to family, you don't count the cost.

As much as all that was true, I wanted to be realistic. If anything went wrong at any point, we both knew that the total could easily exceed £10,000. When I'd told people at the end of the race that I wanted to bring Gobi home, Allen, Richard, and quite a few other runners had all said they wanted to help and would make a donation. In the days after I got home, I received more than a few e-mails from competitors at the race, asking how they could give money to the Gobi fund. I knew that Gobi's courage and determination had touched many people, so it wasn't surprising that they'd want to hand over a few pounds to help make sure that she had a good, safe life ahead of her.

So Lucja and I sat at the computer and set up a crowdfunding page. When it came to putting in a target, we both paused.

"What do you think?" she said.

"How about this?" I said, typing in "£5,000" on the form. "We'd never get it, but it's probably the most realistic estimate of how much it's going to cost to get her here."

"And if we get only a few hundred pounds, it'll help."

Over the next twenty-four hours, my phone chirped a few times to tell me that a handful of donations had come in. I was grateful for each and every gift from my fellow runners, knowing that even a few pounds given here and there made the task ahead a little bit easier. More than the money, however, I loved reading the comments people wrote. Helping Gobi made them happy. I hadn't quite expected that.

I also didn't expect the phone call Lucja received on the second day after the crowdfunding page went live. The guy introduced himself as a journalist and said he'd seen the crowdfunding page and asked to speak to me. He explained how he'd found Lucja's number on her site that promotes her as a running coach. It felt a bit weird to know that a stranger could track us down like that, but when he explained why he was calling, I was intrigued.

He wanted to interview me and write an exclusive feature about Gobi for his newspaper, the *Daily Mirror*.

Journalists from papers such as his don't always have the best reputation. A few years earlier the *Daily Mirror*, along with several other papers, had been caught up in a phone-hacking scandal, and trust was still low. But the guy sounded genuine enough, so I decided to say yes and see what would happen. At the very least, it might be fun to post it on Facebook and get a few more people reaching for their wallets.

Before the call ended, the journalist reminded me that it was an exclusive and that he was concerned I might talk to other journalists and give them the story before he had a chance to publish.

"Mate," I said, then laughed. "You can do what you like with the story; no one else is going to care about it."

We did the interview by phone the next day. He wanted to know all about the race and how I'd met Gobi, how far she'd run with me, and how I was hoping to bring her back. I answered all the questions, and though I was a little bit nervous at first, I felt okay with how the interview went.

I didn't know whether to be anxious or excited when I went to buy a copy of the paper the following day. I skimmed through the pages, wondering what I was going to find.

What I didn't expect was a full page with great photos from the race and a really good write-up. But that's what I saw, sitting beneath the bold headline: "I Will Not Desert My Ultra-Marathon Pal." The journalist got all the facts right, and he even had a quote from the race founder, who said, "Gobi really became the race's mascot—she embodied the same fighting spirit as the competitors." I liked that.

I'd been in a paper before, when I finished sixth in my first ultra, and I'd had a few mentions on race blogs and in a few running magazines, but this was a whole other level. It was weird but in a good way, and I quickly put messages up on the crowdfunding site, Facebook, and anywhere else I could think of. I thought it would be a pretty good encouragement for anyone who had already made a donation.

I had checked the crowdfunding page as I went to pick up the paper that morning. It was at almost £1,000, with about six or seven people having donated. An hour after I put the paper down and started making my third coffee of the morning, something amazing happened.

My phone went wild.

It started with a single notification. Someone I'd never heard of had just donated twenty-five pounds. A few minutes passed, then came another message, telling me someone else I'd never heard of had given the same amount. After a few more minutes, there was another. Then another. Then someone gave a hundred pounds.

I was astounded and even a little confused. Was this real?

A few more pings and a few more minutes passed, and I checked on the Internet to see whether the article in the paper was also on the *Daily Mirror* site. It was there all right, and in the few hours that it had been live, it had been shared and liked by hundreds of people.

I'd never imagined anything like this could happen.

The online version of the article described the story as the "Heartwarming bond between ultra-marathon man and the stray dog he refuses to leave behind".[1] Something happened in me when I read those words. I'd known all along that my heart had been

1 Jonathan Brown, "Heartwarming Bond Between Ultra-Marathon Man and the Stray Dog He Refuses to Leave Behind", *Mirror*, 27 July, 2016, updated 28 July, 2016, www.mirror.co.uk/news/real-life-stories/heartwarming-bond-between-ultra-marathon-8507261.

warmed by Gobi and that I refused to leave her behind, but I'd not used those words with the journalist. It was his description, and the fact that he had seen the significance of my meeting Gobi in much the same way that I did was encouraging.

Maybe that's why people are making these donations, I thought. *Maybe they see what he saw too.*

Twenty-four hours after the piece came out in the paper, the crowdfunding page showed that the £5,000 target had been met. But it didn't stop there. People kept on giving, all of them strangers to Lucja and me, all of them somehow moved by the story of this little dog who for some unknown reason chose me and wouldn't give up.

As well as constant updates about the donations, my phone started to pop with messages from other journalists. Some of them messaged me through the crowdfunding site, others through social media or LinkedIn. It was hard to keep track of them all, but I wanted to get back to every one of them.

The UK papers contacted me first—another tabloid, then a couple of the mainstream papers. I suspected that the approach the journalists took would vary from paper to paper, that perhaps they might want to know about different aspects to the story. But they were all happy to ask the same questions: Why were you running in China? How did you meet Gobi? How far did Gobi run? When did you decide to bring Gobi home? Will you run with her again?

The first time I heard that last question, it made me stop. I realized that in all the busyness and planning, I'd never thought about what life would be like when Gobi came home to Edinburgh. Would she expect twenty-five-mile walks each day? How would she cope with city living? And if I did ever run with her again, would she stick to my side as she had before, or would she want to head off by herself into this strange new world with all its distractions?

There was so much I didn't know about Gobi's past, and there was so much I didn't know about our future together. I guess that's what makes the start of all relationships so exciting—even the ones with scruffy stray dogs.

After I'd had a few interviews with different newspapers, I got a message from someone at the BBC. Phil Williams wanted to interview me for his show on Radio 5 Live later that night, and even though I was starting to feel a bit tired from all the talking, no way was I going to turn him down.

The interview turned out to be the best thing I could do at the time. The producers combined the audio of my interview with video footage they'd managed to get from the race. The little one-minute video was more popular than I think even they imagined. Before long it had been viewed 14 million times, making it the second-most-viewed video on the BBC site.

After that, things really took off.

I did interviews with other BBC shows and stations; then the TV people started calling. I spoke with other channels in the UK, then ones in Germany, Russia, and Australia. I got on Skype and did interviews with CNN, ESPN (where Gobi's story was in the top-ten plays of the day), Fox News, ABC, the *Washington Post*, *USA Today*, the Huffington Post, Reuters, the *New York Times*, and podcasts, including the *Eric Zane Show*, which, in turn, gave the story a boost to a whole other level.

All along, the total on the crowdfunding page just kept rising. People from all over the world—Australia, India, Venezuela, Brazil, Thailand, South Africa, Ghana, Cambodia, and even

From the moment I carried her in this position through the river crossing, Gobi has loved being in my arms.

My heart has never forgotten my first dog, Tilly. When my family moved from Roma to Warwick, we had to leave her behind with a farmer.

I was five in this photo; those skinny legs would come in handy one day.

I loved bike riding, moving as fast as I could, and I taught Christie how to ride too.

Garry and me at eight—within a year, it would never be the same again.

My skinny legs kept getting longer, and I started to play cricket and hockey.

My grandmother was my last connection to any real, loving family.

Deon Hansen was my best mate when we were growing up.

My sister and mother were with me on Lucja's and my wedding day in Italy.

I was sucking in all the water I could during that 2013 155-mile race in the Kalahari Desert.

I had a surprising smile on my face, thanks to Lucja's being with me after a run in the 2013 Kalahari race.

On day one of the 2014 race across the Kalahari Desert, I was gunning for the lead.

Day six was another marathon in the 2014 Kalahari race.

I nailed the long stage (nearly fifty miles) in six hours and fifty minutes in the Kalahari race in 2014.

I enjoyed a little bit of coolness with the temperature at 122 degrees in the 2014 Kalahari Desert race.

Lucja and I were proud as punch of each other in the 2014 Kalahari Desert: she finished second in the women's race, and I finished second in the men's.

I completed a non-stop sixty-two-mile race in the Gobi Desert in 2016.

Urumqi was plastered with these reward posters when Gobi was lost.

Where next? The search team and I worked out our next location to search for Gobi.

We bloody well found her—one of the best nights of my life!

I hosted a celebration dinner for the Ma family and all the volunteers who helped in the search for Gobi.

Richard and I celebrated Gobi's return.

Gobi and I met Chris for the first time in Beijing. Chris had been instrumental in directing the search party and offering advice to find Gobi.

Gobi and I did some sightseeing outside Beijing at the Great Wall.

Gobi was feeling sorry for herself after that hip operation to mend the injury she suffered in Urumqi.

The time immediately after Gobi's operation was tough for both of us.

While staying in Beijing, I often had to wear a pollution mask.

Kiki was the most amazing woman: she did everything possible to help Gobi and me in Beijing and organized our next steps to meet the requirements for departure.

Once all the requirements were met, Gobi and I were finally ready to leave China and start our journey home to the UK.

Time to fly! Gobi and I started the countdown, leaving Beijing for Paris.

Even though it took longer than imagined, I kept my promise to get Gobi to the UK and had a great feeling upon our arrival.

Chilling together on Arthur's Seat, Gobi and I were still in complete amazement that we were finally home.

Lucja, Lara, Gobi, and I celebrated our first Chinese New Year together as a family.

Gobi and I had our first run together on UK soil in my home city of Edinburgh, Scotland.

North Korea—pledged to give what they could to the cause. Their generosity was humbling as well as exciting. I'd been to some of these places, and I knew the kinds of lives a lot of the people in them lived.

Within the space of a few days, everything had changed for Lucja and me. We'd been a little unsure about whether to do the crowdfunding and felt aware of just how big a challenge it was going to be to get Gobi home. In the space of twenty-four hours, nearly all of that concern was wiped out. Having Kiki's support and getting so many pledges from people meant that we knew beyond doubt that the biggest obstacles had been taken care of: we had the expertise to get her back and the funds to make it happen. Everything seemed to be falling into place.

Almost everything.

Nurali wasn't answering any of our e-mails.

12

"I JUST DON'T SEE IT, LUCJA. I DON'T SEE HOW it's going to happen."

We were lying in bed, waiting for the alarm, having our first conversation of the day, but the words had an eerie familiarity about them. I'd said the same thing many times in the week that had passed since the *Daily Mirror* article came out. While the crowdfunding page was up to almost £20,000, all we were getting from Nurali was silence.

Every time Lucja and I talked like this, I had tried my best to explain what I knew of Nurali and Urumqi. I had told her how the city was this crazy, busy place, and everyone there was rushing around doing their stuff. "Nurali thrives on being busy, so I can't imagine she's sitting at home with her feet up. She's probably got a hundred other projects going on, and there's no way she's going to take time off to help us. Looking after a little dog has got to be way down her list of priorities."

"So we need to remind her that this matters. We need her to remember how important this is, don't we?" said Lucja.

I remembered the night of the sandstorm. "Nurali's one of

those people who won't help if she thinks you're being a pain. If we stress her out, I reckon she'll go even slower just to piss us off."

We sat in silence for a while.

"Do you think she's seen all this stuff on Facebook?"

There was no way that would have happened. With no Facebook or Twitter making it into China, and almost no Western news channels on TV, I couldn't imagine how any of the buzz we were experiencing had made it back there.

"So what do we do?"

Silence settled on the room again. The conversation always came undone at this point. We were stuck, unable to get out. We were powerless to make anything happen. We could do nothing other than wait.

Even though Nurali was silent, the rest of the world was not. Along with Kiki's e-mails asking if we still wanted her to help, we started to see an increasing number of comments on the Facebook page asking for updates. People, rightly so, were wondering what was going on. They wanted to know how the process of getting Gobi ready to travel was going and when she was coming home. They wanted photos, video, and news.

I couldn't blame them. If I'd have given money to a cause like that, I'd feel the same way. I'd want to know the dog was being looked after and the owners were acting diligently and responsibly. I'd want evidence that everything was moving forward. I'd want to know the whole thing wasn't a scam.

Though Lucja and I were desperate to provide people with the reassurance they wanted, we couldn't do it. All we could do was post vague messages about how everything was in hand and we were taking the first steps in what was going to be a long, long journey. We rationed our news and photos the way we rationed our food on a long desert stage.

A few more days slipped by, and still we received no response from Nurali. I could tell that Kiki was finding all this waiting a bit frustrating, but she clearly understood the unique nature of the challenge ahead of us. She offered to e-mail Nurali herself, and we gladly agreed. Hopefully the fact that Kiki was Chinese would solve any language and cultural problems.

The supporters, on the other hand, were getting more vocal, and more and more requests for information were being made. I began to worry that if we didn't come up with some concrete news soon, the huge wave of positive support might back away from us. Worse still, people might turn against us. So I decided to call one of the race organizers.

"This is a big deal now," I told her. "It's not just me who cares about bringing Gobi back; it's gone global. It feels like thousands and thousands of people are watching and wanting to know what's going on. The ones who have donated are like shareholders, and they want answers."

She listened and told me that she understood. "I'll make it happen," she said.

When the call ended, I felt a weight fall from me. If the race organizers were going to get involved, we'd be fine. They masterminded a whole series of races that took place on four different continents; surely they could get a little dog reunited with her master.

Sure enough, Kiki got an e-mail from Nurali a week later. Everything was fine, though Nurali did agree that there was a lot more to be done than she had first anticipated. She and Kiki agreed that Nurali would keep on looking after Gobi, but that Kiki would send someone out to Urumqi to take care of everything that needed to be done before Gobi could fly back to Beijing.

This was good news. But the process was taking so much longer than either Lucja or I had hoped. What mattered most was that Gobi was safe, Nurali was still taking care of her, and Kiki would soon have someone in Urumqi putting the plan into action.

Nurali even e-mailed some pictures, and we were able to give the supporters a full progress update. It did the trick and answered most of the questions people had. The press inquiries kept on coming, and I spoke with magazine journalists for the first time as well as more radio stations.

For the first time since arriving home from China, I felt truly confident that everything was going to work out.

The next week, however, I started to get nervous. Nurali had gone silent again. It was so frustrating. Two weeks had dragged by since we launched the crowdfunding site, and we were no closer to getting Gobi the medical care and tests she needed to begin the process of flying her back home.

I e-mailed the race organizer again to see if she could help, but instead of getting a reply from her, I received one from her office. They said she was in America, as was Nurali. They wrote that Gobi was being looked after and that Nurali would be back in China in a few days and all was good. They passed on a message saying that the organizer planned on talking everything through with Nurali when they were together.

Lucja and I didn't know what to think. We were a bit annoyed that it was going to be yet another week until Kiki could get someone out to see Nurali and get things moving, but we had known there could be speed bumps along the way. And who knew, maybe Nurali would catch some of the coverage of the story when she was in America and get a clearer picture for herself of how much attention Gobi was getting.

Nurali was as good as her word. When she was back in China a few days later, she e-mailed Kiki and promised to get things happening quickly.

Great, I thought, when Kiki told me the news. *Not long now.*

A day later I checked in with Kiki: Any word from Nurali on when you can send your person out to Urumqi?

Her reply was quick.

Dion, I have not heard back from Nurali. Kiki.

I waited another day.

Any news today, Kiki?

Again, Kiki got straight back.

No.

I e-mailed the race organizer again: Why's this all taking so long? Don't tell me something's happened.

The next day, Kiki had nothing to report, and my inbox didn't get anything from the race organizer either.

Another day passed, and from the moment I woke up, I knew something wasn't right. Sitting in bed, waiting for the alarm again, I was as wired as if I were already on my third coffee. I couldn't tell Lucja exactly what I thought was wrong. "But there's a problem," I said. "I just know there is."

I got up and checked my phone, knowing it was already late afternoon in China. Among the handful of e-mails from journalists and the great pile of notifications from the crowdfunding page, one stood out:

> **To: Dion Leonard**
> **From: **** ******
> **Date: August 15, 2016**
> **Subject: Gobi**
> **Dion, I need to ring you.**

When the race organizer and I spoke later that morning, there was a part of me that wasn't surprised by what I heard. She told me that while Nurali had been away in the United States, her father-in-law had been looking after Gobi. She'd run away for a day or two but come back for food. Then she had gone missing again and hadn't returned at all. Gobi had been missing for several days now.

"You've got to be kidding me," I said. I was trying to remain calm and not explode with a barrage of expletives. I was bloody furious. "What are they doing to find her?"

"Nurali's got people out there looking. They're doing their best to find her."

Doing their best? I had serious doubts about that and was upset that Gobi had been able to escape. I'd had so much time to think about Gobi, I'd run every possible scenario through my head. I was paranoid. The version of events that the organizers were relaying didn't seem quite right to me. Nurali had been quiet for so long, I was worried Gobi had gone missing a lot earlier, and they didn't tell me about it because they thought they would find her. If I was right, that meant Gobi had already been on the run for ten days or more.

All kinds of scenarios flashed across my mind. None of them were good, and I did my best to shut them out. This was no time for panic. I needed to act.

"So what can we do?" I asked, not having a clue what should happen next.

"Nurali's doing all she can."

Somehow, that didn't seem like enough.

I phoned Lucja at work and told her that Gobi had gone and that I seriously doubted whether Nurali was looking for her as had been suggested. Then I phoned Kiki and went through the story all over again.

"Let me speak with Nurali," she said. That was the first suggestion I'd heard all morning that made any sense.

When she called back, Kiki told me she had her doubts about the whole story. It just didn't add up.

"Okay," I said, putting my suspicions aside for a moment. "But what's next?"

"What we need to do is get more people involved in the search."

"How can we do that? Nurali's the only person I know in Urumqi."

"I know someone here in Beijing who has experience finding dogs. He runs an adoption shelter in Beijing. Maybe he can help."

I didn't have to wait long for Kiki to call back a second time. She had spoken to her friend Chris Barden from Beijing's Little Adoption Shop, and as I listened to the advice she relayed, I knew he was the right man for the job.

"First, we need a poster. It has to have recent photos of Gobi, a good description of her, and the location where she went missing. It needs a contact number and, most important, a reward."

"How much?" I asked.

"He says five thousand RMB to start."

I did my calculations. Five hundred pounds. I'd gladly pay ten times that if we needed to. After giving it some thought, I settled on £1,000 for the reward.

"We have to get the poster everywhere, especially digitally. Do you have WeChat?"

I'd not heard of it, but Kiki filled me in on the WhatsApp/Twitter hybrid that the Chinese authorities did not block.

"Someone needs to set up a WeChat group to start sharing the news. And then we need people on the street handing out the posters. Chris says that most dogs are found within two to three miles of the place they went missing. That's where we need to concentrate all our efforts."

The thought of putting this plan into action and expecting it to work made my head spin. I knew from experience that Gobi could easily cover two or three miles in twenty minutes, so she could be way beyond Chris's boundary. But even if I put that to one side, I couldn't imagine where Gobi might be because I had no idea where in the city Nurali lived. All I knew for sure was that Urumqi was about as densely packed as anywhere I'd been in Asia. A two- or three-mile radius could contain tens—if not hundreds—of thousands of people. Nurali was my only hope for getting the word out on the street, but I didn't know if she could do it.

Thankfully, Kiki saved the best news until last.

She told me that Chris knew someone who lived in Urumqi, a woman called Lu Xin. When her own dog had gone missing, Chris had helped with the search. He'd already asked her, and she said she'd help, even though she'd never led a dog search before.

I exhaled a great breath of gratitude.

"That's amazing, Kiki. Thank you so much." I was blown

away by the kindness of these people I'd never even met, who had jumped into action at a moment's notice. I hadn't prayed since I was a kid, but I certainly said a few words of thanks right there and then.

I went back to waiting for news. It was lunchtime in Scotland, but the end of the workday in China. I knew I wouldn't hear anything more from Kiki until the next morning.

I'd been home from China for nearly four weeks and had started back at work almost immediately, squeezing in the interviews and e-mails in the early mornings, late evenings, and weekends. I work from home some of the week, and on the other days I'm in the office, down in the south of England. On the day I found out Gobi was lost, I was in the flat, but as the afternoon dragged on, I wished I was anywhere but there. Being at home alone was hard. Harder than running across the black Gobi Desert. All I could think about was Gobi.

When the working day finished and Lucja came home, we talked about what to do. Both of us knew we had to let people know about Gobi being lost, but phrasing it the right way was hard. We knew so little, but we didn't want people filling in the blanks.

After a few false starts, late that night, I finally posted the words I hoped would alert people and help get Gobi back safely:

> Yesterday we received a phone call that Gobi has been missing in Urumqi, China, for a number of days, and she has still not been found. We are simply devastated and shocked to hear that she is now on the streets of the city, and our plans to get her to the UK are up in the

> air. It has literally been the worst 24 hours, and I know that my pain and grief will be shared by you all. Please understand Gobi was well cared for and looked after in Urumqi, and this has been an unfortunate incident.
>
> Today the below information and reward has been released on Chinese WeChat. The Urumqi animal shelter has also kindly assisted in providing a group to look for Gobi, and we are also organizing to employ locals to look for Gobi across the streets and parks of the city.
>
> If anyone can provide any information on Gobi's whereabouts, please contact us as soon as possible. We hope and pray Gobi can be found safe soon and will keep you updated with any progress.
>
> Just like to say we are so appreciative of all the funding and support provided to Gobi so far. I can confirm there are still 33 days to go on the crowdfunding page, and if Gobi is not found during this time, then no money will be taken from the pledges.
>
> Dion

Within minutes I could hear my phone alert me to the responses as they came in. It was slow at first, then faster and faster, like a slow jog turning into an all-out sprint.

For a while I didn't pick up. I didn't want to read what people were writing. Not that I didn't care what they thought. I did care. I cared a lot. But I had no more news to give them, and there was nothing else I could do.

My only option was to sit and hope. Hope that Gobi was still okay. Hope that this woman Lu Xin—whom I'd never even heard of before I woke up that morning—would work miracles and build up a big enough search team to flood the area with posters so that someone somewhere who had seen Gobi and who cared enough to act would phone in and claim the reward.

Who was I kidding? There was no hope of success.

As the last light of the summer evening slipped from the sky, my thoughts turned darker. I remembered something else that Kiki had told me during our last call of the day. She said that Chris met Lu Xin when her own dog went missing. He was the one who had advised her on the search.

Lu Xin's dog was never found.

PART 4

13

THERE'S BARELY AN AUSTRALIAN ALIVE WHO hasn't heard of the ultra-runner Cliff Young. The man's an inspiration to all of us, not just endurance athletes. To anyone who has ever faced an insurmountable challenge that nobody believes can be overcome, Cliff's story offers hope.

On Wednesday, 27 April, 1983, Cliff Young turned up at the Westfield shopping mall in the western suburbs of Sydney, looking for the start line to a remarkable race. The route led to another Westfield shopping mall, 543.7 miles away in Melbourne.

The race was widely considered to be the toughest of its kind, and the assembled field included some of the best in the world, men in their prime who had trained for months to reach peak physical condition for the event.

Cliff stood out from the handful of runners who had gathered for the brutal race. He was sixty-one years old, wore overalls and work boots, and had removed his dentures because he didn't like the way they rattled when he ran.

While most people assumed he was either a spectator or a

maintenance guy who'd gotten slightly lost, Cliff collected his race number and joined the other runners.

"Mate," said one of the journalists when he saw Cliff on the line, "d'you think you can finish the race?"

"Yes, I can," said Cliff. "See, I grew up on a farm where we couldn't afford horses or tractors, and the whole time I was growing up, whenever the storms would roll in, I'd have to go out and round up the sheep. We had two thousand sheep on two thousand acres. Sometimes I would have to run those sheep for two or three days. It took a long time, but I'd always catch them. I believe I can run this race."

The race started, and Cliff was left behind. He didn't even run right; he had this weird-looking shuffle where he barely lifted his feet from the ground. By the end of the first day, when all the runners decided to stop and get some sleep, Cliff was miles and miles behind them.

The pros knew how to pace themselves for the run, and they all worked the same plan of running for eighteen hours a day and sleeping for six. That way the fastest among them hoped to reach the end in about seven days.

Cliff was working with a different plan. When they resumed the race the next morning, the other runners were shocked to hear that Cliff was still in the race. He'd not slept and had shuffled his way right through the night.

He did the same thing the second night as well as the third. With each morning came more news of how Cliff had jogged through the night, breaking down the lead that the runners half his age tried to stretch out in the day.

Eventually Cliff overtook them, and after five days, fifteen hours, and four minutes, he crossed the finish line. He had broken the record by almost two full days, beating the five other runners who finished the race.

To Cliff's surprise, he was handed a winner's cheque for $10,000. He said he didn't know that there was a prize and insisted he had not entered the race for the money. He refused to take a cent for himself and instead divided it equally among the other five finishers.

Cliff became nothing short of a legend. It was hard to know what footage of him people loved most: the shots of him shuffling along highways in slacks and a casual T-shirt or the images of him chasing sheep around the pasture, wearing gum boots and a look of pure determination.

I was a kid when the Aussie news networks covered Cliff's story. He was a celebrity, a genuine one-of-a-kind who had done something amazing that made the whole nation take notice. It wasn't until I became a runner myself that I appreciated how remarkable his achievement was. And it wasn't until Gobi went missing and I found myself on a flight back to China that I returned to his story and drew inspiration from it.

The day after I posted the news that Gobi was missing, we were flooded with messages from people all over the world. Some were positive and full of sympathy, prayers, and good wishes. Other posts expressed fears that Gobi would eventually end up being eaten. It was the first time I'd ever thought about the possibility, but it didn't strike me as very likely. Even though I'd spent only ten days in China, I had a feeling that the rumour of the Chinese as dog eaters was probably off the mark. Sure, I'd seen stray dogs around the place, but I'd seen the same in Morocco, India, and even Spain. Instead of being cruel, every Chinese person who'd taken an interest in Gobi had treated her with care and affection, nothing less.

While I appreciated people's warm wishes and could handle their panic, there was a third type of message that I just didn't know what to do with:

> How the hell did that happen?! Seriously????

> I knew something like this would happen . . . What a horrible place for that dog to be lost too. I'm disgusted for how this was handled.

> How on earth was the dog able to escape????

> These "caregivers" had one job to keep this precious small dog safe and these [supposed] guardians failed her! . . . How do you lose a dog you were supposed to be watching until she could be ADOPTED!

I felt bad. In fact, I felt terrible. So many people had given so much money—about £20,000 by the time she went missing—and now Gobi was gone. I knew that in the eyes of the public I was fully responsible for Gobi. I accepted that and knew the blame stuck with me.

If I'd handled things differently, Gobi wouldn't have gone missing. Yet what else could I have done? When I finished the race and left Gobi with Nurali, I assumed it would take only a few weeks before we'd be reunited in Britain so Gobi could begin the quarantine process. Had I known how hard it was going to be to get her across China and then out of the country, I would have hired a driver and taken Gobi back to Beijing myself. But all I knew, at the time I finished the race, was that Nurali—who seemed to me the very best person for the job—was happy to help. At the time it seemed enough.

I was tempted to reply to each message, but they were coming in even faster than they had after the *Daily Mirror* article had hit. Every few minutes there was a new comment, and I knew that it was best just to give people the space they needed to vent their anger. There was no point in getting drawn into any arguments.

Besides, there was another type of comment that started to get my attention.

> I wonder if it's a kidnap situation due to all the publicity surrounding her story.

Even though I can get annoyed with people when they mess up, I'm generally a very trusting person. I'd never thought of Gobi's escape as anything other than an accident. The more I read of these messages, however, the more I started to wonder.

> I hope this wasn't intentional or that someone wasn't behind this. Forgive my suspicion, but I don't understand how this could happen! Gobi's story went global, and I just hope someone (not Dion) isn't trying to make money off taking her. Missing for days, and you were just notified?

The comments did make a good point. Thousands of people around the world were following the story, and the crowdfunding total was visible to all. Was it hard to imagine someone trying to make some easy money by dognapping Gobi and hoping we'd pay a reward for her safe return?

I was supposed to be working, and I tried my best to get on with the reports I had to write, but it was hard going. I must have spent most of the day distracted by all these thoughts and questions. I felt like a feather in a storm: powerless and at the mercy of forces far, far stronger than me. By the time Lucja came home from work, I was exhausted.

She'd been following the feedback throughout the day, and while I had been sidetracked by the posts that looked for someone to blame, she'd been struck by the ones that tried to find a solution:

> Can you fly there to look? She'll feel you and find you! Please use the funds to keep her safe until she flies home with you. This is devastating.

> She is looking for you. Heartbreaking. I am praying she is found safe. I don't think anyone would think twice if you used some of that crowdfunding money to offer a reward for her safe return. Has this been put out to the media outlets to get the word out?

I'd been home for six weeks and had about the same amount of time left before going to another 155-mile race in the Atacama Desert in Chile that October. I'd not picked up any injuries in China, and I'd been able to resume my training almost as soon as I got home. I was convinced that I was going to be in the best possible condition to go out and win Atacama, especially now that

I knew some of the runners I was going to be up against, such as Tommy and Julian. And if I won Atacama, I'd go to Marathon des Sables in 2017, ready to score a top-twenty place. In the whole history of the race, no Australian had ever finished higher.

Making a sudden trip to China to search for a lost dog was not part of my training plan. Six weeks out from Atacama, I should have been clocking one hundred miles a week on the treadmill in my improvised homemade sauna. Instead, I was doing nothing. All my training had fallen away as the search for Gobi overtook my life.

Putting Atacama aside, I had other good reasons for not going back to China. I'd hardly been at my best at work in the previous weeks, and asking for even more vacation time without giving my employers any notice would be pushing their goodwill to the absolute max. If I were in their position, I knew exactly what I'd say.

And if I did go, what could I honestly hope to achieve? I couldn't speak the language, I couldn't read Chinese, or whatever version of Arabic it was that I'd seen in Urumqi, and I had even less experience searching for lost dogs than the woman who was leading the search. If I went, I'd be wasting their time as well as mine.

In the end it didn't take long for me to change my mind. It wasn't that all my doubts were suddenly answered or that I had a profound sense that if I went, I'd find Gobi. I decided to go because of a simple, compelling fact I shared with Lucja late on the second night after I'd been told Gobi was missing: "If I don't go, and we never find her, I don't think I'd ever be able to live with myself."

And so it was that I found myself sitting by a departure gate in the Edinburgh airport, ready to embark on a three-flight, thirty-plus-hour journey back to Urumqi. I snapped a photo of my flight itinerary and posted it online. With so many people being kind and generous in the previous days, I wanted them to know I was doing all I could to help.

Only four days had passed since the phone call, but I flew with the knowledge that the people who had given so generously to help bring Gobi home wanted me to go back and find her. We had set up a second crowdfunding site, called Finding Gobi, to pay for my travel as well as the costs that the search party was already incurring—printing, gas, drivers, staff, and food. As with the Bring Gobi Home site, people's generosity had left both Lucja and me speechless. We smashed our target of £5,000 within the first couple of days.

I went with the blessing of my boss as well. When I'd started to tell him that Gobi had gone missing, he didn't wait for me to finish. "Just go," he said. "Find the dog. Sort it out. Take whatever time you need."

As for Atacama, that was the one problem to which I couldn't find a solution. I knew that going back to China would be pushing my time-off allowance at work and meant cancelling my plans to race in Chile, but I decided there was no use worrying about it. If I lost Atacama but found Gobi, all would be worthwhile.

I boarded and checked Facebook one final time. Dozens of messages had come in, all of them full of encouragement, positivity, and good faith. Many of the comments said the same thing: these people were praying for a miracle.

I agreed. That was exactly what we needed. Nothing less would do.

Somewhere in the sleepless fog of the all-night flight, the story of Cliff Young came into my mind again.

Like me, he had no idea that he was going to cause such a stir when he ambled up to the start line in 1983. I'm guessing he didn't have a clue that he was going to win it either. But he knew he could make the distance. Experience, self-belief, and a little bit of not knowing what he was up against all helped give him the confidence he needed.

Was I going to find Gobi? I didn't know. Was I going to be able to do what people suggested and get the local media to cover the story? I didn't know that either. Did I have any experience of ever having done anything like this before? None at all.

But I knew I had the heart for the fight. I knew my desire to find Gobi was as strong as any desire I'd ever had within me. Whatever it took, I knew I wasn't going to rest until there was nowhere left to search.

14

TEN MINUTES AFTER WE DROVE AWAY FROM the airport, I finally worked out what I didn't like about Urumqi. I'd been too distracted to notice when I came through the city as I'd been travelling to and from the race, but as I sat in the back of Lu Xin's car next to the translator, I listened to her explain the reasons why every street light and bridge was covered with closed-circuit TV cameras. I finally understood. Urumqi felt oppressive. It felt dangerous. In an odd way, it reminded me of living in the hostel in Warwick when I was fifteen. The threat of violence was all around, and I felt powerless to defend myself.

According to my translator, Urumqi is a model for how the Chinese state tackles political unrest and ethnic tensions. There's a history of violence between the indigenous Uighur people, who practise Sunni Islam and who see themselves as separate from mainstream China, and the Han Chinese people, who have been encouraged by the Chinese state to migrate into the area with the incentive of tax breaks.

In 2009, Uighur and Han took to the streets, fighting each

other with iron pipes and meat cleavers. More than one hundred people died, and almost two thousand were wounded.

"You see that place?" asked my translator, whom I nicknamed Lil. She was a local girl who happened to be studying English at the university in Shanghai. When she heard about Gobi, she signed up, and right from the start I connected with her.

We had hit traffic and were crawling past a wide patch of open ground bordered by razor-wire fence and guarded by soldiers holding automatic weapons at the entrance. The soldiers were carefully watching people as they lined up to pass through an airport scanner. To me, it looked like a military facility.

"That's a park," Lil told me. "Have you been to one of the train stations here?"

"Oh yeah," I smiled. "That was fun trying to get through. What are there, two layers of security to go through?"

"Three," said Lil. "Two years ago Uighur separatists launched an attack. They used knives and set off bombs. They killed three and injured seventy-nine. Then, a few weeks later, they killed thirty-one and wounded ninety at a market."

In the wake of the 2009 violence, the Chinese authorities installed thousands of high-definition closed-circuit TV cameras. And when the knife attacks, bombings, and riots resumed a few years later, they installed even more, as well as putting up scanners and miles of razor wire and flooding the streets with heavily armed soldiers.

Lil pointed out a new police station that was being built on a tiny scrap of land, then another identical one under construction farther down the road. "This month we have a new Communist Party secretary. He was the top official in Tibet, so he knows how to manage ethnic tension. All these new police stations and security checks are thanks to him."

I didn't think Lil was being sarcastic, but I couldn't be sure. As she continued talking, I got the sense that she thought little of the Uighur people.

"When Communist forces arrived in the Xinjiang region sixty years ago, Chairman Mao put the clock forward permanently. He wanted every region to be on the same time as Beijing. But Uighur people resisted, and their restaurants and mosques still run two hours behind. When Han Chinese wake up and start work, most Uighur are still asleep. We're like two different families living in the same house."

It was all very interesting, but I hadn't slept on the flights. All I wanted to do was get to my hotel and hibernate for a few hours.

Lil said there wasn't time for the hotel.

"Lu Xin wants you to meet the team. They spend the afternoons looking in the streets around where Gobi went missing and handing out posters. We'll take you to the hotel later."

Ever since I'd heard about Gobi's disappearance, I'd been frustrated at what seemed to be a lack of action, so I couldn't complain now.

"All right," I said, as we pulled up at a traffic light alongside an armoured vehicle packing enough firepower to take down a bank. "Let's do it."

When we parked at the top of a residential street and I finally saw the area where Gobi had gone missing, my heart sank. Blocks of flats eight or ten storeys high lined the street. Traffic surged along the main road behind us, and in the near distance I could see an area of scrubland that looked like it led all the way off to a series of mountains in the distance. Not only was the area densely packed with people and dangerous traffic, but if Gobi had decided to head for familiar territory and run off in the direction of the mountains, she could be miles and miles away. But if she'd stayed in the three- to five-mile radius as Chris had suggested, we'd have to knock on thousands upon thousands of doors.

I'd not talked to Lu Xin much in the car, but as I stared about, she stood beside me and smiled. She started talking, and I looked to Lil for help.

"She is telling you about when she lost her dog. She says that she felt just like you do now. She also says that Gobi is out there. She knows it, and she says that together we will find her."

I thanked her for her kindness, although I couldn't share her optimism. The city was even bigger than I remembered, and one look was enough to tell me that the area that Nurali lived in was full of places a dog could go missing. If Gobi was injured and had found somewhere safe to hide, or if she was being kept against her will, we'd never find her.

Lu Xin and Lil were deep in conversation as they led the way down the street. I followed on behind with the rest of the search team: a handful of people about my age, mainly women, all clutching posters and smiling eagerly at me. I nodded back and said *nee-how* a few times, but conversation was limited. I didn't mind so much. Somehow the prospect of finally being able to walk the streets and put up some posters—to actually *do something* for once—made me feel better.

We turned a corner, and I saw my first stray dog of the day. It was bigger than Gobi and looked more like a Labrador than a terrier, with teats hanging low on the ground, like a sow.

"Gobi?" queried one of the ladies next to me. She was wearing a white lab coat and clutching a stack of posters; she smiled and nodded eagerly as I stared back at her. "Gobi?" she asked again.

"What? Oh no. Not Gobi," I said. I pointed to the pictures of Gobi on the poster. "Gobi small. Not big."

The woman smiled back and nodded with even more enthusiasm. I felt the last ounce of hope evaporate like steam.

We spent the rest of the afternoon walking, putting up posters, and trying to calm down the woman in the white coat—who Lil told me was a doctor of Chinese medicine—whenever she saw a dog of any kind.

We must have looked like a strange collection of freaks as we followed behind Lu Xin and Lil—the sensible, normal-looking ones. There was me, the only non-Chinese I'd seen since leaving the airport, standing a foot taller than anyone else, looking worried and sad. Alongside me was Mae-Lin, a particularly glamorous woman (a hairdresser, apparently) who carried herself like a 1950s movie star and was accompanied by a poodle with blue dye on its ears and a summer skirt around its waist. Then there was the woman whom I nicknamed "the doctor", with her perpetual smile and eager cries of "Gobi? Gobi?" which she shouted as she ran off down random alleys and around the back of blocks of flats. When the strays got close, the doctor would reach into her pocket and pull out some treats.

It was obvious that all of them loved dogs, and as we walked and talked with Lil, I learned why.

"Stray dogs are a problem in China," she said, translating for Lu Xin. "Some cities will round them up and kill them. That's how they get into the meat trade. But that doesn't happen here—at least, not in public. Most Uighur think dogs are unclean, and there's no way they would have them as a pet in their house, let alone eat them.

"So the dogs roam the streets. They can sometimes be dangerous, so people kill them. That's what we're trying to change. We want to look after the strays, but we also want to show people that they don't need to be scared of dogs and they should look after them too."

I was sure that Nurali was a Uighur, and I didn't quite know how to take Lu Xin's news.

"Do you think Nurali would have looked after Gobi well?"

Lu Xin looked awkward.

"What is it?" I asked.

"We've been talking to people, and we think Gobi might have gone missing before Nurali thinks she did. We think Gobi may have escaped earlier."

"How much earlier?"

She shrugged. "Maybe one week. Maybe ten days."

I'd suspected as much all along, but it was still painful to hear. If Gobi really had been missing for so long, the distance she could have covered was vast. She could be far, far away from the city by now. And if she was, I'd never find her.

All throughout the afternoon we saw strays, but they were always alone. They avoided the main roads and trotted down the side of the quieter ones. It was like they were trying to keep themselves out of sight.

It was only after a few hours that we saw our first pack of strays. They were sniffing around a patch of bare earth a few hundred feet away, and because I was tired of walking and wanted to cut loose and run for a while, I told my fellow searchers that I was going to head off and quickly check them out.

It felt good to run.

When I reached the place where the pack of dogs had been, they'd already scattered. The patch of land wasn't totally empty, and in one corner there was a half-finished cinder-block structure. Instead of turning around and going back to rejoin the others, I decided to poke around.

The weather was so much hotter in August than it had been at the end of June, and the sun was fierce that afternoon. I guess that was why there weren't any other people around and the noise of the traffic had subsided. I stood in the shade of the half-built building, enjoying the stillness.

Something caught my attention. It was a familiar sound, one that took me back to the day when Lucja and I went to retrieve Curtly, our Saint Bernard.

I went around the back of the building in search of the source.

I found it soon enough.

Puppies. A litter of two, maybe four or five weeks old. I watched for a while. There was no sign of their mum, but they looked well enough. Even though Urumqi was clearly not a haven for pets, the dense housing meant that there must have been plenty of opportunities for a dog to scavenge food.

With their big eyes and clumsy paws, the puppies weren't just cute; they were adorable. But as with all mammals, that helpless, cuddly phase would pass. I wondered how long they'd have before they would be forced to fend for themselves. I wondered whether they'd both make it.

I heard the others calling my name as I approached them. They were clearly agitated, and the doctor ran out to grab my hand and hurry me back to Lil.

"Someone has seen a dog they think is Gobi. We need to go."

I didn't know what to think, but there was a buzz in the air.

Even Lu Xin was looking hopeful, and as we drove the half mile to the location, the chatter in the car became increasingly animated.

By the time we got there, I was starting to believe it too. Then again, I probably would have believed anything; I hadn't slept properly in thirty-six hours, and I couldn't remember the last time I had eaten.

An old man holding one of our posters introduced himself to Lil as we parked. The two talked for a while, the old guy pointing to the picture of Gobi on the poster and indicating that he'd seen her some way down a track that ran around the back of a block of flats.

We went where he suggested. I tried to tell people that their habit of calling out "Gobi! Gobi!" as we walked was pointless, given that Gobi had been known by that name for only a few days. She was smart but not that smart.

Nobody took my advice, and the cries of "Go-bi! Gooooo-bi!" continued. After thirty minutes of wandering, I was beginning to tire. The surge of adrenaline I'd experienced when the news of the sighting first came in had long gone, and I was ready to call it a day and get to the hotel.

The flash of brown fur a few hundred feet ahead stopped us all in our tracks. There was a moment of collective silence. Then chaos erupted.

I ran hard towards the dog, leaving the sound of the others calling out far behind me. Could it really be Gobi? The colour was right, and it looked like the same size as well. But it couldn't be her, could it? Surely it couldn't be this easy?

The dog was nowhere to be seen when I got there. I carried on searching, running down the network of alleys and dirt paths that connected the blocks of flats.

"Gobi? Gobi! Dion! Dion!"

The shouting came from behind me, somewhere back near the main path.

I raced back.

The searchers were gathered in a knot, crowding around. They parted as I approached, revealing a tan-coloured terrier. Black eyes. Bushy tail. Everything was a match. But it wasn't Gobi. I knew it from ten feet away. The legs were too long and the tail too short, and I knew from looking at the dog that it had none of Gobi's spirit. It was sniffing around people's feet as if their legs were tree trunks. Gobi would have been looking up, her eyes digging deep into whatever human happened to be close at hand.

The others took some convincing, but eventually they accepted it.

The search would have to continue.

Back in the hotel, in the minutes before my body gave in to the deep tiredness that had been growing all day, I thought back on the afternoon.

The members of the search team were wonderful people—dedicated and enthusiastic and giving up their time for no financial reward whatsoever—but they didn't have a clue about Gobi. They were searching a whole city that was full of strays for a single dog, and all they had to go on was a home-printed poster with a couple of low-quality images.

They'd never seen her in person, never even heard her bark or watched the way her tail bobbed about when she ran. What chance did they have of recognizing her in a city like this?

Finding Gobi was going to be like finding a needle in a haystack—maybe an even greater challenge than that. I was an idiot for ever thinking that I'd be able to do it.

15

YOU COULD SAY I'M AN ADDICT. THE FEELING I get when I'm in a race, when I'm right at the very front, is a powerful drug. At some races, like the Marathon des Sables, if you're the guy at the head of the pack, you'll have a car ahead of you, helicopters tracking you from the air, and a whole load of drones and film crews capturing your moment in full high-definition glory. It's fun, but the real buzz doesn't come from all that horsepower and technology. What gets me fired up is the knowledge that behind me is a herd of one thousand runners—all running a little bit slower than me.

I've spent a couple of days running like that in Morocco, and I've been fortunate enough to compete in a heap of other races too. Every time I'm one of the front runners, whether there are choppers overhead or nothing but damp-looking volunteers sheltering from the Scottish weather, the high stays with me for days afterward.

In fact, I don't even have to be in first place to get my win-junkie fix. I'm also a realist, and I know that I'm never going to win a race like the Marathon des Sables. Those top-ten slots are the preserve of the most gifted endurance runners on the planet. I'm just a hobby runner who came to the sport late in life after a decade of life as a fat bloke stuck on the couch. Against professional athletes who have spent their lives running, the odds are never in my favour.

That means I must set my goals carefully. At an event where the best in the world are running, *winning*, for me, is a top-twenty finish. The buzz I'd get from finishing that high up the table at Marathon des Sables would be every bit as sweet as an Atacama gold spot.

I'm thankful that in the few years I've been running, I've become well acquainted with the highs of my sport. I also know the lows, and there's nothing I hate more than being unable to compete. Being injured to the point where I can't move as quickly as I think I should really kills me. Being overtaken by people I know I'm faster than hurts like a knife in my heart. Being so down on myself that I choose to stop and bail on a race entirely, as I did on my very first ultra, is about as bad as it gets.

Those experiences can leave me feeling drained and depressed. I get angry with myself and frustrated to the point of wanting to throw it all away. In those times I'm not much fun to be around.

Searching for Gobi on the hot summer streets of Urumqi, I could feel the crash coming. I could tell it was going to be a big one.

I'd been on a high since finishing second in the Gobi Desert race. Part of that was the success of the run, part was the continued success in my training, and a whole lot of it was thanks to the excitement about bringing Gobi home. As soon as she went missing, I kicked into action mode—first working out how to find her, then how to tell the supporters, then how to get myself out to Urumqi to join in the search. Life had been frantically busy right from the moment of that dreaded phone call, and I'd not had a chance to stop.

All that changed once I arrived in Urumqi. When I woke up for the first time in the hotel, the reality of the situation finally caught up with me. I was convinced all was lost.

I knew I needed to put on a brave face for the rest of the search team, so when Lu Xin came to collect me soon after breakfast, I put on my sunglasses and my biggest smile and tried to pretend that everything was fine.

We spent the morning resuming our poster campaign, working systematically along the streets and putting a poster on the windscreen of every parked car that we could see. More often than not, if we returned to the street an hour or two later, we'd find all the posters removed and piled up in a rubbish bin.

We had a couple of arguments with the guys whose job it was to keep the streets clean. The first time it happened, the old man wouldn't listen to Lu Xin's attempts at an explanation. The second time it was the doctor who stepped up. She faced off with another old guy, and this one was putting his heart and soul into the shouting. Flecks of spit were flying from his mouth as he ripped up a handful of the posters that he'd swiped from the first few cars. The doctor got up in his face, shouting just as loud. They were both speaking so fast that I didn't bother asking Lil to translate, but I could tell the doctor was refusing to back down.

Eventually she won. The old man took a good hard look at me, put up his hands, and backed away. The doctor's performance was as much of a surprise to the others as it was to me, and we all stood, staring in awe when she turned back towards us.

That was about the only good moment of the day. The rest of the time I spent trying not to let my thoughts spiral away from me.

It was almost impossible. All it would take would be a glimpse of the mountains in the distance, and I would worry that Gobi had tried to head back to the kind of terrain with which she was familiar.

Midway through the afternoon there was another flurry of activity as news of a possible sighting came in. Someone had sent a picture this time, and it was clear to me that the dog looked nothing like Gobi. I was all for giving it a miss, but the rest of the team wanted to check it out. After the previous day's letdown, I was surprised the team was still so positive.

The dog wasn't anything like Gobi, of course, and I went back and sat in the car as soon as I could. I probably looked as though I was desperate to keep going, and, in a way, I was. But all I really wanted was just a moment's rest. Wearing the fake smile was killing me.

By the time Lu Xin returned me to the hotel, it was late at night. We'd got rid of thousands of posters along miles and miles of parked cars. We'd argued with street cleaners, begged with shopkeepers, and seen countless drivers return to their cars and throw the posters to the ground without even looking at them. I had not eaten since breakfast, was still jet-lagged, and was told that the hotel restaurant had already shut down for the night.

I ordered some room service, took a drink from the minibar, and tried calling Lucja. No reply. So I waited some more and took another drink. Then another.

When Lucja called back, a great surge of sadness flowed out of me, like water down a drain after the plug is pulled after a bath. I couldn't talk for a minute or more. All I could do was cry.

When I finally caught my breath and wiped my face, Lucja had some news for me. She'd been e-mailing Kiki since I left

Edinburgh, and they'd both agreed that with me in Urumqi now, we needed to do all we could to get the local media to cover the story. She had spent a lot of the day getting in touch with outlets, and after a lot of communication difficulties, she had arranged for one of them to come and interview me the next day.

"It's just a local TV show," she said. "It's not much, but it's a start. Maybe it'll kick things off, like the *Daily Mirror* article did."

"I hope so," I said. We both knew my heart wasn't in it.

"Hey," she added. "Someone on Facebook said that you need to make sure those posters aren't just in Chinese but are also in whatever language the Uighur read. You've done that, haven't you?"

"No," I sighed, eyeing another drink. "Lucja, this whole thing's impossible. If she went farther into the city, there's traffic everywhere and great packs of stray dogs that would probably rip her to pieces. If Gobi went out to the mountains, she could be a hundred miles away by now, and even if we could somehow know what direction she went in, there are no roads to follow. All we've done is hand out posters, and now we find out that none of the locals can read them. We're finished even before we've begun."

Lucja knows me well enough to let me rant a while longer. Only when I'd run out of words did she speak again. "You know what I'm going to say, don't you?"

I did. But I wanted to hear her say it anyway.

"Sleep on it. It'll all look different in the morning."

For once Lucja was wrong. I didn't wake up feeling optimistic, and we didn't have any breakthroughs as we continued the search in the morning. We went through the usual routine of distributing posters, getting into arguments, and dealing with the depressing sight of those mountains in the distance.

There was one difference, however: the search team was now

considerably bigger. Along with Lu Xin, Lil, the hairdresser, and the doctor, many others had now joined our team. At one point, later during the search, I counted fifty people, twenty of whom chose to search all through the night while I was sleeping. They were remarkable people, and I could never thank them enough.

Doing the TV interview in the hotel later was a good idea. It reminded me of the surge of interest that we'd had back when the fund-raising kicked off. I'd not done any interviews since Gobi had gone missing, mainly by choice. With no news to share, there didn't seem to be much point.

The local TV station was different. The reporter wanted to know why a guy from Scotland would come all the way to this city to search for a dog, and he seemed to like the fact that the search was being led by locals.

Whatever the station did with the story, it worked. The next day we had two new volunteers join the search and more than a dozen requests for interviews from Chinese TV stations and newspapers. Just like the *Daily Mirror* and BBC coverage back home, that first Chinese TV interview had gone viral, unlocking interest from all over the country. One TV station even sent a crew along to follow me for a two-hour live broadcast of the search out on the streets.

Not all the attention was positive. Lu Xin took a call from a woman who claimed she had seen Gobi in a vision and that Gobi was running through snow-capped mountains. I dismissed it out of hand, but I could tell that a few of the searchers were interested.

So I said, "Tell her if she's any good at having these visions, she needs to have one that has a bit more detail in it. We need to know exactly which one of these mountains Gobi is in."

I knew nobody was going to get the joke.

The following day the new posters arrived, with the message in both Chinese and whatever version of Arabic the Uighur use. We got the same disinterested reaction from people, but at least the media interest continued to rise.

People started coming up to me on the street wanting to have their photo taken. My lack of Chinese and their lack of English meant we'd hardly ever be able to talk much, but they all seemed to have heard about Gobi and wanted to take a few posters with them. Every time that happened, I reminded myself that if this all worked out right, it was only going to take one poster to do it.

Along with the Chinese media, the international outlets started to get interested again. Lucja had worked the phone hard at home, and after a day's searching in the streets, I'd get back to the hotel and speak to journalists and producers in the UK and the US. It meant staying up late and not getting much sleep, but it was a whole lot better than sitting around feeling powerless and depressed.

Ever since I arrived in Urumqi, I'd been relying on Lu Xin and her team. We had no offers of help from the authorities or other organizations. We were on our own—that much was clear.

Over the years a lot of people have told me that—given the way my childhood turned sour—they are surprised I'm not messed up. I tell them my childhood contained some hardship, but it also gave me the tools I needed to survive. All that pain and loss gave me a certain kind of toughness, and running gave me the chance to put it to good use. Pain, doubt, fear. I discovered that I'm good at blocking them all out when I'm running. It's as though I have a switch I can flip on or off at will.

I use that blocking ability at work too. I don't give up when it looks like all is lost, and I won't take no for an answer. That mental toughness I learned as a kid has helped me in many ways. I'm grateful for it. But losing Gobi was a shock. It taught me that I'm not as tough as I think.

After everything she had done to stick with me, I couldn't just forget about her. I couldn't flip the switch and move on. I couldn't stop myself from fearing the worst, from doubting our chances, or from feeling the tremendous pain of knowing that—day by day—I was losing her.

16

DAY FOUR IN URUMQI WAS ALMOST IDENTICAL to all the others. I was up at six o'clock, eating dumplings with the rest of the search team in a café in a converted shipping container. We were talking about how long Gobi had been missing: officially it had been ten days, but none of the volunteers believed that. They all thought she'd been missing for at least twice that.

A new girl joined us, Malan—bringing our number that morning up to ten. Malan told me that she had seen me on TV the night before and was so moved by the story that she contacted Lu Xin and asked if she could come along and help. She proved her worth right from the start, suggesting we distribute the Uighur-language version of the poster in a nearby Uighur neighbourhood.

The homes were all single storey, a patchwork of loose bricks and rusted metal roofs. Every other street we'd been down had been wide and clean and lined with cars parked on the side. This Uighur neighbourhood had narrow, twisting alleys, few cars, and a lot of goats caged up in spaces not much bigger than a hotel bathroom.

I wondered if this was the first time in the Uighur part of town for the Han Chinese members of the search party. If it was, they didn't show it. They just got on with the job of putting posters into as many hands as was physically possible.

The only difference in the day came in the afternoon when Lu Xin left me at the hotel to do another interview while she drove to the airport to pick up Richard, my tent mate from the Gobi race. He lived in Hong Kong, and his work took him all over China. He and I had kept in touch since the race, and he'd been a generous supporter of the Bring Gobi Home fund-raising. When he found out that he was going to be a short flight away from me in Urumqi, he offered to come and help with the search for a few days.

I was excited about having a friend come and join me, and the fact that Richard was fluent in Mandarin was another bonus. I was also looking forward to being able to run. Ever since arriving in Urumqi, I'd ambled around the streets at the same tortoise-slow pace as the rest of the search team. I'd tried getting them to pick it up a bit, but it was no use.

Richard and I went for a run in a park near the hotel as soon as he came back from the airport. I'd had my eye on the mountains all along and had seen several villages in the scrubland that separated the city from the hills. I wanted Richard to help me cover some miles and hand out a bunch of posters among the locals up there.

Richard had other plans. I didn't know it at the time, but Lucja had been in touch with him already, asking him to look after me because she knew I was stressed and not eating properly.

After the run, we met up with the team. Lu Xin looked anxious as Lil told me about a few phone calls she'd taken. That was nothing new. The more posters we'd hand out, the more calls we'd get. Mostly they were false alarms, but sometimes they were from people asking if we would increase the reward if they brought Gobi in. They were time wasters, and after the first few, Lu Xin stopped telling me about them.

These calls were different. I could tell she was hiding something. I pressed her to tell me what was going on.

"Just someone being bad," she said. But I wasn't satisfied.

"Tell me. I want to know."

"Lu Xin took a call this afternoon. They said that Gobi is going to be killed."

At first I didn't get it, but as the news sank in, I felt sick. If this was a joke, it was despicable. If it was real, I was terrified.

I'd calmed down a bit by the time I returned to the hotel, but the interview with BBC Radio later that evening was a bit of a disaster. I was feeling particularly hopeless and depressed about the search, and even though I knew how important it was to sound upbeat and positive, to make it clear that this was not a hopeless case, I failed. I was exhausted, worried, and unable to see how we could ever hope to find Gobi. It was not my finest media hour.

Even though I'd been feeling so flat, I'd wanted to do the interview because of a piece that had appeared in the Huffington Post two days earlier. Under the headline "Missing Marathon Dog Gobi May Have Been Snatched by Dog Meat Thieves", the piece quoted someone from Humane Society International who said that it was "very worrying that Gobi has gone missing in China, where between 10 and 20 million dogs are killed each year for the dog meat trade".[1] From everything that Lu Xin had told me, the dog meat trade was not common in the region we were in, especially

1 Kathryn Snowdon, "Missing Marathon Dog Gobi May Have Been Snatched by Dog Meat Thieves, Humane Society International Warns", Huffington Post, 22 August, 2016, www.huffingtonpost.co.uk/entry/gobi-missing-marathon-dog-may-have-been-snatched-by-dog-meat-thieves-humane-society-international-warns_uk_57baf263e4b0f78b2b4ae988.

given the large number of Muslim Uighur who lived there. There was no way they would ever eat a dog, which they considered to be as unfit for human consumption as a pig.

Not only was the piece inaccurate, but it was also not helpful. We had our small band of dog lovers joining in the search, but we needed the local and national Chinese media to cover the story and help convince the wider population in the city to care about a little dog. Chris and Kiki had already advised me to stay positive and never say anything critical of the state while I was being interviewed, and I knew that if the authorities felt that the story was being used by the Western media to paint the Chinese as dog-eating barbarians, I'd lose all hope of ever getting their help again.

The truth was that the local search team had been great. I wanted to tell the BBC and all the supporters back home what amazing support we'd received from the general public as well as the authorities. I wanted to make it perfectly clear that everyone I'd met had been helpful, kind, and generous. I couldn't have asked for more from the team, the Chinese media, and Kiki back in Beijing. Even if we never found Gobi, their support had been phenomenal.

That's what I wanted to tell the BBC that night. Instead, I sounded as though I was ready to end it all.

Richard rescued the situation with a few beers and a good meal. We talked about things that had nothing to do with Gobi or the search, and Richard told me he was a former US marine. He wouldn't tell me any more than that, although when the conversation did return to Gobi, he had some interesting theories on what had happened to her.

"None of this adds up," he said. "Even without those calls, it still looks wrong to me. I don't think it's got anything to do with Nurali being in the US or her father-in-law accidentally letting her escape. I think that the moment Gobi's story went viral and the fund-raising kicked in, someone spotted a chance to make some money. That's all this is about, Dion—money. This is a shake-down. The call will come."

I wasn't so sure. Part of me didn't believe him because I couldn't imagine anyone would go to such lengths for just a few thousand pounds. Then there was a part of me that didn't believe him because I just didn't want to. I couldn't stand the thought that Richard might be right and that Gobi's survival depended on whether some idiot thought he could get enough money out of us to make it worthwhile. What if Gobi's captor changed his mind? What if he got cold feet? Would he return her carefully to Nurali, or would he treat her like any other failed business experiment and dispose of her as quickly as possible?

My phone buzzed with a message from Lu Xin.

Look at this photo. Gobi?

I wasn't convinced. The quality of the image was poor, but what I could see of the eyes didn't look right at all. Plus, there was a deep scar on the dog's head that Gobi didn't have during the race.

I sent a quick reply saying that it wasn't Gobi, but Richard wasn't so sure.

"Don't you think we should go and have a look?" he said.

I was tired and tried to brush him off. "Mate, we've had almost thirty of these, and they're always the same. It'll take an hour and a half to get up there, see the dog, have a chat, and then get back. It's getting late, and we've got to be up early tomorrow."

Richard looked at the photo again. "Looks a bit like Gobi to me."

Lu Xin sent another message thirty minutes later. This time it was a better-quality image, and someone had enlarged the eyes and pasted them next to the photo of Gobi from the reward poster. Maybe she and Richard did have a point.

Richard was convinced when I slid the phone over to him. "We've got to go," he said.

We drove into the gated community and parked in between a shiny Lexus and a couple of BMWs. A whole bunch of the cars had foot-long red ribbons tied to one of their wing mirrors—a sign that the cars hadn't long left the dealership. The neatly tended gardens and wide apartments themselves spoke of wealth. This was clearly one part of Urumqi that I'd not seen.

As we followed Lu Xin, I told Richard that we were wasting our time. And as the front door of the residence opened to reveal every single person in the search team, plus another ten or more strangers I'd never laid eyes on, I couldn't help but sigh. Any hope I had of being out of here quickly and back to bed was blown out of the water.

Because of the crowd of people, I couldn't see much, and the noise was intense too. I couldn't even tell where this Gobi look-alike was at first, but as I pushed a little deeper into the room, a knot of people at the back stepped aside and a streak of sandy brown shot across the room and jumped up at my knees.

"It's her!" I shouted, picking her up and thinking for a moment that I'd slipped into a dream. She soon started making that same excited, whimpering, yapping sound she'd made whenever I'd been reunited with her at the end of a day apart on the run. "This is Gobi! It's her!"

I sat on the couch and took a good look at Gobi. Her head didn't look like I remembered it. There was a big scar across it, a mark as wide as my finger running from near her right eye back behind her left ear. I knew she didn't know her name, but whenever we'd been on the run or in the camp, all I had to do was make a little clicking sound, and she'd come straightaway. So I put her down on the ground, took a step to the other side of the room, and clicked.

She was by my side like a shot. It was her all right. There was no doubt in my mind. No doubt at all.

The noise levels in the room exploded. People were shouting and calling out her name, but I wanted to check Gobi over and make sure that she was okay. I found a couch and looked again, running my hands up and down her back and legs to check. She winced when I touched her right hip, obviously in pain. She was okay to stand and could put some weight on it, but between the hip and her scar, I knew she was lucky to be alive. Whatever had happened to her, it had been quite the adventure.

Gobi was burrowing into my lap like a newborn puppy, and the others crowded around for photos. I understood their excitement, and I was so grateful to them for their help, but it was a moment that I really would have enjoyed being alone. Well, just Gobi and me.

The doctor got a little overexcited and wanted a selfie with Gobi. She picked her up and must have touched her hip, because Gobi let out a loud squeal of pain and jumped out of her arms and back into mine. After that, I didn't let anyone else get too close. Gobi needed some protecting, even from the people who loved her.

It took an hour for the hysteria to calm down and the full story to emerge. Richard translated while Mr Ma, the house owner, explained how he had found her.

He'd been in a restaurant with his son earlier in the evening. His son had been telling him about this girl he'd seen that afternoon—the newest member of the search team, Malan. She had been putting up posters that she'd added handwritten messages pleading with people not to throw away the posters because it was sad that the dog was missing and a man had come all the way from the UK to find her. Mr Ma's son had thought that was a kind thing for her to do.

As they walked home from their meal, they saw a dog, looking hungry and tired, curled up at the side of the road.

"That's the same dog, Dad," he said. "I'm sure of it." He made his father wait while he ran back a couple of streets to where they'd passed some of the posters.

When they called out to Gobi, she followed them the short walk home, where they then phoned the number on the poster and sent the photo to Lu Xin. When she relayed my message that I didn't think it was a match, it was Mr Ma's son who scanned the poster, took a better-quality photo, and made it clear how similar the eyes were. He was convinced even if I wasn't.

"So what do we do next? We take her back to the hotel, right?"

Richard translated. Then both he and Lu Xin shook their heads.

"They won't let you. No hotels in the city will ever allow a dog in."

"Really?" I was shocked. "But after all this? After all she's been through?"

"They're right," said Richard. "Maybe you can try and talk to the manager and see if he'll let you, but I doubt it. I stay in hotels all over, and I've never seen a dog in one."

It was past eleven o'clock, and I was too tired to argue, either with my friends or with a hotel receptionist.

"We should ask Mr Ma to keep her here tonight," said Lu Xin. "Then you can buy all the things you need for her, like a lead and collar, food, bowls, and a bed, and then collect her tomorrow."

Lu Xin had a point. I'd been thinking so long about Gobi's being lost that I'd never come up with a plan for what we should do when we finally found her. I was totally ill equipped and felt bad at the thought of saying goodbye to Gobi and heading back to the hotel. But the others were right; it was the only sensible option.

I looked at Gobi, curled up beside me on the couch. She was going through that same twitch and snore routine that she had on the first night she slept beside me in the tent.

"I'm sorry, girl," I said. "I've got a lot to learn about being your dad, haven't I?"

On our way back to the hotel, I rang Lucja. "We bloody well found her!" I said the moment she picked up. Both of us didn't say much for a while. We were too busy crying.

PART 5

17

THE HOTEL MANAGER WAS A STRANGE GUY.

I had spent enough time driving around the city to know that the hotel was one of the very best in Urumqi. He'd let us use one of the meeting rooms downstairs to carry out numerous interviews, and the story was all over national TV. So I was convinced that if I asked nicely, he'd do us a favour. I thought he'd bend a couple of rules, if he had to, and let Gobi stay in the hotel. Surely the guy would understand how an opportunity like this would be good for business.

"No," he said.

His English was better than that of most people I'd met, but I tried repeating the request, a little slower this time.

"Can the dog stay in my room? She's only little. It'll be good publicity for you."

"No," he said again. He understood perfectly what I was asking. "We don't ever let dogs stay in the hotel." He paused a moment, then spoke again, his voice lowered. "But I would be willing to help."

I did some internal high fives. Even if it cost me a few hundred pounds, I knew it would be worth it to keep Gobi safe.

"Perhaps the dog could stay in one of the rooms that we use for staff training."

It didn't sound ideal, but I didn't have many other options. "Can I see it?"

"Of course," he said. "This way, please, Mr Leonard." Instead of taking me deeper into the hotel, he led me out of the revolving front door, past the security guard with the standard-issue bulletproof vest and rifle, across a busy car park, and through a set of doors that didn't appear to have any locks at all on them and swung in the breeze, like saloon doors from an old-time western.

That wasn't the worst part. The room itself was a disaster.

It wasn't so much a training facility as a dumping ground. The place was full of cleaning bottles and broken furniture. The door itself didn't appear to be closable. The manager saw me looking at it and tried to shoulder it shut as well as he could, but there was still a Gobi-sized gap at the bottom where she could easily crawl out.

"I can't keep her in here," I said. "She'd run off."

"So?" he said, turning away and walking back out into the car park.

Like I said, he was a strange guy.

Richard and I had already been out first thing and bought a selection of Gobi essentials in the sprawling market beyond the hotel car park. There wasn't much choice, but we managed to buy a lead and collar, a couple of bowls, and some food. And as we walked, we hatched a plan for what we'd do if the hotel manager turned us down. And it looked like we'd have to resort to Plan B.

Back at Mr Ma's, Gobi was just as excited to see me that morning as she had been the night before. I was relieved about that and to see also that Mr Ma obviously had looked after her well. In all the chaos of the night before, I'd not forgotten that Richard suspected there was some foul play at work. But the more I talked to Mr Ma and saw that he was a regular guy who dressed as if he were going to head to the gym but not actually do any work, the more I trusted him. And when I found out he was a jade dealer, that did it for me. He obviously didn't need the money. There was no "shakedown" going on here.

I told Mr Ma that I wanted to give him his reward at a special dinner we were going to hold for the search team the following night. He agreed to come along but insisted he didn't want the reward money. Just as Richard, Lu Xin, Gobi, and I were about to leave, another man—wearing what looked to me like a fake smile—entered the house. I'd not met him before, but he did look familiar.

"I am Nurali's husband," he said, as he shook my hand with what felt like an iron grip. I knew he meant business.

I remembered where I'd seen him. He was one of the drivers at the race. Gobi was down on the ground, and he knelt to pick her up.

"Yes," he said, turning her around in front of him as if she were an antique vase that he was considering buying. "This is Gobi all right."

He handed her back to me. "We tried our best to keep her safe for you, but she escaped. She's going to need a good fence when you get her home."

Our plan for getting Gobi back into the hotel was simple. We were going to put her in a bag and carry her in. The trouble was, like all hotels and public buildings in Urumqi, there was more to security than a guy with a bulletproof vest and an AK-47. There was an X-ray machine and a walk-through metal detector to negotiate.

It was up to me to play the fool and create a diversion. I had an unzipped bag full of posters and snacks that I dropped on the floor near the scanner. I made a big fuss and apologized profusely as I crawled around the floor picking them up. Meanwhile, Richard—with Gobi sitting silently in a bag made of denim that looked a little like a coat—walked right through the metal detector, hoping he'd remembered to remove anything that would set off the alarm.

Back in my room, it was finally time to check out Gobi. The scar on the top of her head told the story of a nasty wound, and I wondered whether it had been inflicted by another dog or a human. It was thick, but the scab was well formed, and I didn't think I needed to worry about it too much.

Her hip, though, was a problem. She clearly had been in pain when the doctor had picked her up awkwardly the night before, and even when I put the lightest pressure on it, she twitched away. But it was when I put her down to walk that the problem was the most obvious. She could barely sustain any pressure on it at all.

Again I was left wondering what had happened to her.

I'd spoken to Kiki that morning about what needed to happen next. We knew Nurali hadn't made a start with any of the medical requirements that Gobi needed in order to fly, so the first priority was getting her to a vet. After that, it would be a question of waiting for the paperwork to be completed and the travel to Beijing to be authorized.

"How long will that take?" I asked.

"Maybe one week, maybe one month."

I felt a little of yesterday's depression return. "Are you sure we have to fly? Why don't we drive?"

"It's a thirty-hour drive, and no hotel will let you take her inside with you. Would you really want to leave her in the car?"

I wouldn't. We agreed that driving would be the back-up plan.

"Besides," she added, "I have a contact at an airline who says she might be able to get Gobi on the flight without any trace of her being on it."

For the rest of the day, I did the only thing I could and looked after Gobi. I fed her when she was hungry, let her wrestle with my socks when she was bored, and snuck her down in the lift to the basement car park when she needed to do her business. She was the dream dog; she didn't bark in the room, and she didn't mind going back in the bag when I took her out of the room.

In a strange way the experience reminded me of the one time in my teenage years when I felt close to my mum. I was ill and needed taking care of, and for a while all that was toxic between us evaporated.

The illness flared up when I was thirteen, lying on the carpet at home, waiting for the biggest TV event of my lifetime to happen. The cute girl and cool boy in a popular Aussie soap opera called *Neighbors* were about to get married. It was all everyone could talk about—bigger even than Cliff Young's winning the Sydney to Melbourne run. I was in love with Charlene, the cute girl, and took my front-row space on the carpet as the opening music started. "Neighbors, everybody needs good neighbors . . ."

Just as Scott and Charlene were about to say "I do," I blacked out. That's all I remember.

When I woke up, I was in a hospital. I felt terrible, like everything inside me had been rearranged the wrong way. The doctors were using words I didn't understand, and I couldn't hold on to a single thought properly. A terrible feeling of nausea raged within me. For hours I felt as though I was about to explode, until I finally fell asleep and woke up twelve hours later.

I had had an epileptic fit, and Mum had to explain epilepsy to me.

I had seizures a few more times, and each one was followed by a period of a day or two when I'd feel terrible. I had to stay out of school, visit specialists, and deal with the prospect that this unexpected visitor to my life could return at any time, bringing chaos with it.

And then, less than a year after that first attack, I began to realize that months had passed since my last attack. The doctor appointments became less and less frequent, and life returned to normal.

The funny thing was, I almost missed having epilepsy. Not the attacks themselves but the way in which they turned the clock back on things with my mum. With each attack came a softening in her, a new kind of warmth. The harsh words disappeared, she cooked my favourite meals, and she even gave me cuddles. Having lost Garry the way she had, seeing me in the middle of an epileptic seizure must have been hard for her, but all I received from her was love and care. Those were precious times. Finally, I had my mum back. Sadly, that didn't last.

I tried to care for Gobi the way I remembered my mum caring for me. I tried to let go of the stress of the previous few weeks and just enjoy spending time with her. It helped that we were both exhausted, too, and spent a lot of that day dozing together.

The next morning I had a problem. Gobi had all the food she needed right there in the room, but I wanted something other than dog biscuits and tinned meat for breakfast. Because Gobi was sleeping, I decided to creep out and head down to the ground floor for a quick bite.

I pulled the door shut as silently as I could, hung the "Do Not Disturb" sign on the handle, and crept down the corridor to the lift. As I watched the doors shut in front of me, I wondered whether I would hear a dog bark.

I was back upstairs on my floor in less than fifteen minutes. Striding out of the lift, I passed a cleaning trolley, turned the corner, and saw immediately that the door to my room was open. I ran in. There was no sign of Gobi at all, not under the bed, in the closet, or behind the curtains.

"Gobi!" I was calling, trying to keep the panic out of my voice.

My brain searched through possible scenarios. The hotel manager must have arranged for her to be taken. I ran to the main door and was about to head back to the lifts when I noticed that my bathroom door was shut. I opened it, and there she was, sitting in the tub, head cocked inquisitively to one side, watching the housekeeper wipe down the counter. Gobi looked at me briefly, a kind of "Hey, Dad, what's up?" kind of look.

The housekeeper didn't seem too worried and said a few words as she continued working. I did the only thing I could think of and pulled out my wallet and handed her a 100-yuan note—about ten pounds. I mimed not saying anything about Gobi. She nodded, pocketed the money, and went back to cleaning.

Maybe she wasn't surprised to see the dog there, and maybe she thought the tip was to clean the bathroom extra well. I had no way of knowing. She stayed a long time, cleaning everything in sight. I didn't want to be out in the room since the door to the hallway was standing open, so I stayed in the bathroom, trying to keep out of the cleaner's way with Gobi on my lap. Every time she moved on to clean another part of the room, Gobi and I would have to find a new place to perch.

"Thank you," I said each time we shifted, hoping that she would get the message. "Goodbye. You can go now."

She never got the hint. Instead, she'd just nod, shooing me and Gobi to move from the edge of the tub to the toilet, or from the toilet to the corner behind the door, as she cleaned.

Gobi thought it was all great fun. She sat happily, her tail swatting the air, her eyes darting back and forth between me and the housekeeper.

This has to be the strangest scene ever, I thought.

18

I WEDGED THE DUVET AND PILLOWS FROM THE bed against the door, hoping that if Gobi did make a noise it wouldn't be audible out in the corridor. There was no way I was leaving the room again until I absolutely had to.

I spent the rest of the morning on my phone. I was sending messages to Richard, telling him about the incident with the housekeeper, and to Lu Xin, asking her to look into alternative accommodation options. I spoke to Paul de Souza, a literary agent and film producer in California. He had first heard about the story from his daughter, and he was helping me negotiate a possible book deal. I was amazed at how many publishers had contacted me, but Paul's wisdom and knowledge about the industry were second to none. In between all of that, I was doing Skype interviews with American and British media outlets.

The interviews were fun. Right from the start of the crowd-funding appeal, I knew people wanted to hear about the story because it seemed as though it was heading for a happy ending. Whenever I was interviewed while Gobi was missing, I struggled to know how to adjust to the new questions: How did she go missing? Where did I think she was? Did I fear the worst? I couldn't be upbeat because I didn't have a feel-good story to share. And more importantly, I knew that Gobi's disappearance was shrouded in suspicion. I'd been convinced that something odd had taken place, though I wasn't sure exactly who had taken her. But I chose not to reveal any of this in the interviews. I didn't have all the facts, and it was still too early to be blaming people.

So up in the hotel room, with Gobi asleep on my lap, as I talked to journalists from the *Washington Post* and CBS, things felt right again. I could relax and smile and tell them that I was finally going to be able to repay Gobi's love and determination by giving her a forever home back in Scotland.

Midway through the morning, Gobi woke up, desperate to get outside to do her business. Even though I knew it would happen eventually, I still dreaded the moment when I would have to open the door and peer up and down the hallway to check that the coast was clear.

Thankfully, we had the lift to ourselves as we sank down to the basement level. Gobi trotted off to the same patch of bushes that stood at the car park exit, and I gave her some privacy and looked around.

There was nothing much to see, apart from two men in dark suits stepping out of the lift and walking over to a grey saloon parked nearby.

I was pleased to see that Gobi took a bit of care to kick the dirt back over after relieving herself, but by the time she was finished, the lift doors had opened and out stepped another man into the basement. This time it was a security guard.

It cost me another ten pounds to persuade him to let us

through. I wondered whether it was going to be enough to keep either him or the housekeeper quiet.

Two hours later I found out the answer.

The moment she heard the knock at the door, Gobi started barking. Through the spy hole I could see two men. I recognized one of them instantly—Nurali's husband.

I stalled. What to do? I couldn't pretend I wasn't there—Gobi had seen to that—but how did they find me? One of the hotel workers must have told them which room I was in, but how did they get up to my floor? The only way to operate the lift was by swiping a valid room key. But that seemed to me to be a lot effort on their part, and it did nothing to ease my paranoia.

I sent a message to Richard: *Come to my room immediately.*

"Hello," I said, as I opened the door, trying to crack a smile and appear relaxed and unthreatened. Nurali's husband stared impassively while his friend was trying to look past me into the room.

"Can we come in?" asked Nurali's husband.

I was surprised but curious, so I mumbled "okay" and stepped back from the open door to let them in.

I shut the door behind me and turned around to see them standing over Gobi, looking down. She didn't seem too worried about them, but I doubted they had come just to visit her. Were they here to take her back? Why had they come?

I was about to walk over and pick up Gobi when there was another knock at the door. I saw Richard standing in the corridor, so I opened the door and exhaled a little in relief.

"Hey, man, what do you need?"

"Um, yes, mate," I was terrible at bluffing like this. But I didn't mind. Richard was ex-Marines and having him in the room made me feel a lot safer. More important, he spoke Chinese and could help me get to the bottom of all this. "Didn't you want to come and get some of those posters to take home as souvenirs?"

Richard stayed by the door as I picked up Gobi and waited for Nurali's husband to speak. He fired off a whole load of Chinese and waited for Richard to translate.

Nurali and her husband had seen all the press coverage about Gobi and were worried I would blame them for her escape.

"All I want to do is get Gobi out of here and back home. I'm not interested in trying to find out how she escaped, and I'm not interested in trying to find someone to blame. As far as I'm concerned, it was just an accident, and it's all fine now. It's in all our interests to keep it that way, isn't it?"

Nurali's husband nodded. There wasn't much more to say.

Later that night, after I'd taken Gobi back down to the basement for another ten-pound bathroom break, I watched her fall asleep, then tiptoed out of the room, closing the door silently behind me. I hung the "Do Not Disturb" sign up again and hoped that when I returned a couple of hours later, she would still be there.

It was time to visit the hotel restaurant for the thank-you dinner. I knew I had a lot to be thankful for, and for the next two hours, I was almost able to forget about the events of the day.

The search team had worked harder than I could have hoped for. They had put in long hours in scorching heat and walked mile after mile sticking up thousands of posters. They had been shouted at, ignored, and ridiculed, and they had done it all for a dog they had never even met. Their sacrifice, endurance, and love left me a little teary, and I was honoured to be able to stand up, offer them a toast, and tell them all how deeply grateful I was.

Mr Ma was there, too, with his wife and son. I handed over the reward money, and though he protested a bit at first and seemed slightly confused, after I insisted a few times, he eventually accepted the £1,000.

Midway through the evening I realized that even though I'd been in Urumqi for almost a week and had spent ten days in China for the race, this was my first time socializing with Chinese people. Many Westerners assume the Chinese are serious people, not given to acts of spontaneity. Looking around the restaurant and seeing it full of my new Chinese friends, all laughing, singing, taking selfies, and relaxing, I didn't see anyone who fitted that stereotype.

The doctor was laughing the loudest, Malan was right in the middle of the action, and Mae-Lin, the hairdresser, had turned full-on cougar and was trying her absolute best—but failing—to seduce Richard. I caught Lil and Lu Xin staring at them, and we all laughed even harder.

"I remember when I first heard about Gobi," said Lu Xin.

"When Chris called you?" I asked.

"No. When you were racing. There aren't many news stories about dogs, so whenever there is a story, I always follow it. I knew Gobi was special even then, but I never thought I'd get to meet her."

"You did a lot more than just get to meet her, Lu Xin," I said. "Without you we wouldn't have found her. You're the reason we're all celebrating tonight."

She blushed at the compliment, but I meant every word of it.

She looked up and pointed at the doctor, Mae-Lin, and the others. "Before Gobi, we were trying to care for stray dogs, but nobody listened to us. We were fighting but had no power and no influence. Finding Gobi has changed all that. It's given us a voice. You've helped show that it's right that people should care for animals."

I didn't want to leave, but the longer the night went on, the more I thought about Gobi. I hoped she was still okay in the hotel room on her own. Eventually worry got the better of me, and I headed back upstairs. Gobi was fine, and I did a brief interview with *The Times* before heading back out briefly to find Richard, who was leaving early the next morning.

I knew that having him join the search was going to be helpful, but I didn't know quite how much I was going to depend on him. He didn't just help me keep going when I was at my lowest point; he masterminded the plan to get Gobi into the hotel and gave me some convincing back-up when I thought she might be taken.

I'm a bit of a loner by nature—it's non-negotiable for someone who needs to log a hundred miles or more in training runs each week. But the irony is that some of the strongest friendships I've formed in my life have been formed with people I've competed alongside in ultras. We go through hell on our own out there on the course each day, but the bond that forms is powerfully strong.

When I flew out to Urumqi, I assumed the search was going to be just like another ultra. I thought I'd have to push myself hard, and I expected others to do the same. But in finding Gobi, I found out some valuable lessons for myself as well.

I discovered that working as a team—rather than as a bunch of individuals—wasn't nearly as bad as I used to think it would be. I found out that my areas of weakness were covered by other people's strengths. I didn't have to shoulder the work all on my own. I could lean on the others, and they could take it. They didn't let me down. And I didn't fail them either.

19

EVERY RADIO STATION AND TV NETWORK THAT I had spoken with while the search was in progress wanted a follow-up interview after Gobi was found. In the days immediately following Gobi's return, I gave a total of fifty interviews in person, over the phone, or on Skype. Being that busy suited me. It took my mind off the fear that was growing stronger within me with every hour that passed.

It wasn't just the visit from Nurali's husband or the encounter with the housekeeper that had me worried. In the hotel bar after my *Times* interview, Richard had been sharing his conspiracy theories with me, and all that night my mind had been filled with shady characters lurking in the shadows.

Richard's logic was admittedly compelling. He didn't think Gobi had ever escaped, at least not the way Nurali thought. He said that when the story first went global, someone could have figured out that there was some money to be made from the dog, and when the opportunity arose, they took her. They probably hung on to her so long because the interest kept increasing along with the chance of getting an even bigger payout. But my coming to Urumqi changed things. Suddenly the local press was looking into it, and then the government started taking an interest, with local officials joining the WeChat group. After that, the whole thing became riskier.

"That's why Lu Xin got so many calls saying that Gobi was dead already or that she was going to be killed unless the reward money increased."

"Wait," I said. "What do you mean 'so many calls'? I thought there was just the one phone call. And nobody told me they were asking for more money."

"Yes," said Richard. "They had hundreds of them. They just didn't want to worry you."

I didn't know what to think. Part of me was grateful for their care. Had I known the full story, I couldn't have done anything to help, and I'd have been even more worried. But I didn't like the thought that I'd been scammed.

I was trying to wrap my mind around it all, but Richard hadn't quite finished.

"And don't you think it's weird that Gobi ended up with someone who knew Nurali?"

"So you think the Ma family took her?"

"No. They didn't need the money and wouldn't be interested in taking a dog. But it's quite a coincidence that Gobi was left where people who knew her story could find her. And in a city with mountains and open space nearby, how come Gobi decides to hide on a road near the most expensive gated community for miles? She's not accustomed to high-class living just yet, is she?" It's more likely that the dognappers planted her.

In between interviews the next morning, I messaged Lu Xin to say that I thought it would be best if Gobi and I found somewhere else to stay. Apart from feeling vulnerable in the hotel room on my own, the fact that I couldn't take Gobi freely in and out of the hotel meant that I still hadn't taken her to a vet to get her checked out. If the hip was a problem, it didn't seem fair that she should have to wait. Kiki was still working to get Gobi to Beijing, and I was getting increasingly worried that someone else would try and kidnap Gobi in the hope of a decent reward payout. And besides, every day spent waiting was another day to wait until she could finally come home.

I'd just finished texting Lu Xin when there was a knock at the door. Gobi was in a deep sleep and didn't stir at all, but I still tiptoed across the carpet, my heart jumping and my head spinning.

As I looked through the peephole, I was half-expecting to see the hotel manager standing outside, or maybe a housekeeper who had ignored the "Do Not Disturb" sign. I hoped it wouldn't be Nurali's husband.

It was none of these people.

It was two men in dark suits. I recognized them instantly. They were the same two men I had seen in the basement the day before.

I stepped back from the door, pushing myself flat against the wall. A random movie scene, where a sharply dressed assassin shot the unsuspecting occupant through the peephole, flashed across my mind. I told myself that I was being ridiculous and stole another glance.

They were still there, staring impassively at me.

The door was locked and bolted, and the security chain thrown over, which is how I always have it whenever I'm in a hotel room. I wondered whether I should open it up and see what they wanted. Perhaps they had been sent from the government to make sure Gobi was safe. If that was the case, there was no risk in having a talk with them. But what if they were there to take Gobi, kick us out of the hotel, or exact revenge on behalf of whoever took her in the first place? If any of those were correct, then opening the door was the last thing I should do.

I made up my mind and backed away, keeping close to the wall just in case my thoughts about gunmen and Hollywood movies were some kind of premonition. I hid around the wall by the bed and hoped that Gobi would stay asleep.

Another knock.

It wasn't loud or angry, but it made me hold my breath and freeze. What would I do if they forced the door? Would I pretend I'd been asleep and try and talk my way out of it? Or would I try to use the element of surprise and charge past them with Gobi under my arm and head for the fire exit?

The seconds crept by. There were no more knocks, and they didn't try the handle to see if the door was open. After five minutes I edged back to the door and looked out of the peephole, seeing nothing but an empty corridor. I strained from side to side to see if they might be hiding down low, out of normal sight, but after ten minutes I was convinced they had definitely gone. I carefully pulled away the bedding that covered the bottom of the door and eased the door open. Nothing left, nothing right. I quickly closed, locked, and bolted it again.

I found my phone and sent a message to Lu Xin: **Please, get us out of here! I'm really worried that someone's going to grab Gobi. I didn't sleep all night, and I am really scared for our safety.**

I wanted to get in a car and drive back to Beijing that afternoon, but between Kiki, Chris, and Lu Xin, they came up with a different plan. Kiki's contact said she could help get Gobi permission to fly, and that all we'd need were the basic medical checks carried out by a vet. Once we'd done that, we could be in Beijing in four or five days.

Lu Xin found a flat that I could rent and assured me no one else knew where it was. I didn't want to take any chances. So the next morning I took Gobi down to the basement and handed her over to Lu Xin—the only person in the whole of Urumqi I trusted completely. I was on edge, scanning the parked cars for a grey saloon with two dark-suited males in it. I didn't see it, but that was little comfort to me.

I rushed back up to the lobby, settled my bill, and checked out.

The location of the flat was just as Lu Xin described. I'd not been in that part of the city before, and I was pleased to see that the streets and shops were busy enough to give me and Gobi some cover, without being so crowded that we'd get swamped.

The flat itself was clean and basic, and I felt myself exhale with relief as I said thank you and goodbye to Lu Xin and locked the door behind her.

After Gobi had a good sniff around the entire place, she sat in front of me and looked up into my eyes, just the way she had done on the second morning of the race. It was like she was telling me that she knew something was different but she was okay with it.

"It's quite an adventure we've got ourselves into, isn't it, Gobi?"

She stared back, gave my feet a quick sniff, then trotted over to the couch, jumped up, spun around four times, and curled up in a little ball of sandy-brown fluff.

Gobi wasn't so happy the next day when I took her to the vet. Kiki had arranged for her to be seen by one of the top guys in the city, and I was excited. For the first time in this whole affair, Gobi and I were about to make some real progress towards getting her home.

Gobi didn't agree.

From the moment we got out of Lu Xin's car and walked into the vet's office, Gobi was on edge. She tucked in behind me at first; then as we walked into the examination room, she planted herself on the floor and refused to move.

I laughed it off at first, but once the vet picked her up and started to check her over, I wondered whether she'd sensed something about the place—or the vet himself—that I'd not picked up. He was about as rough and uncaring as any vet I'd ever seen in my life. He pushed and pulled and didn't show any sign of liking dogs in the least.

He told me her hip was displaced and he needed an X-ray to confirm how bad things were.

"Hold her down," he said to his two assistants as he wheeled a portable machine over. They positioned themselves at either end of the table, then grabbed her front and rear paws and pulled back. Gobi squealed, the whites of her eyes showing, her ears pinned back flat against her head. She was terrified and in obvious pain. I tried to protest, but the vet ignored me and carried on with the X-ray.

Gobi was still shaking an hour later as I carried her back into the flat. I was angry with the vet, especially when he showed me the image he'd taken. It was obvious why she had been limping; while her left femur was snug into the hip, her right femur was angled away from the socket, as if it had been bent away with great force. The vet hadn't bothered to explain what might have caused it but told me Gobi would need surgery to correct it. I didn't bother to ask whether it was a procedure he could perform. There was no way he was touching Gobi again.

After a short sleep, Gobi was up and trotting around again. I wondered—as I had a hundred times already—what had happened to her while I was away. Had she been hit by a car, or was it human hands (or feet) that injured her? Only she knew the answer.

Her fear was now clearly gone, and she was ready for some fun. Watching her hop about, keeping her weight off her right leg, as she had ever since I got her back, I was amazed all over again. She must have been in serious discomfort, yet she chose not to complain or let it spoil her pursuit of fun.

I decided to reward her with a little trip outside.

It was a beautiful late afternoon, and she found some good bushes to sniff around in. I wanted to explore the area and see where I might be able to eat later, so I picked her up and carried her as we set off towards the shops.

Within a few feet a couple of twentysomething girls stopped me.

"Gobi?" they asked.

I told them yes and let them take a photo of all of us standing there together. Gobi stared right into the camera like a pro.

A few feet farther on, someone else asked for a photo. I didn't mind, and if Gobi wasn't stressed, I let people make as much of a fuss over her as they wanted. It was great to feel that we were free again.

But when we were twenty feet from the block of flats, I looked across the road and saw it—the grey saloon. It took a moment to sink in, but as soon as I saw the outline of two men in dark suits sitting in the front, I knew the men from the hotel had followed me.

I turned to walk back to the flat. I thought about walking past my block and trying to throw them off the scent, but that was pointless. They must have watched me walk out of the building a few minutes earlier. They had probably been watching me all day. Maybe they even followed me from the hotel.

As I stood in the lift, going up to the seventh floor, the flat didn't feel quite as safe as it had before. I was a little suspicious when the lift stopped on the fifth floor and a man got in. And I didn't think I could trust the woman who was struggling with the lock on her door at the other end of the corridor. Were they all in on it? Or was I just imagining things?

My phone rang as soon as I got back inside the flat, and I jumped at the noise. It was Wendy, an international freelance journalist living in Hong Kong, but it took me a few seconds to register who it was.

"Are you okay?" she asked. "You sound odd."

I told her about the men and the car and how I was getting freaked out by it all.

"That's actually why I'm calling," Wendy said. "It's not just the guys in the car. You've got some pretty big people watching this, Dion."

"What do you mean?" I said.

"Just that—you've got to be careful what you say. I've spoken to some colleagues, and they've heard there are some local government advisers who are watching the story and listening to everything you say. They're okay with what you've been doing so far, but if you criticize the state in any way, they're going to shut this whole thing down. You've got to make sure that anything you say about China is said in a positive way."

"You've talked to people about this? You mean someone's told you this? How could that even happen?"

"Don't worry about how, Dion. I just wanted to make sure you got the message"

"So you think these guys in the suits are from the state?"

"Well, they're not there to steal Gobi, are they?"

I thought about it. Wendy was right. If their intention was to snatch Gobi, they could have done it anytime, and they probably would have done a better job of keeping themselves hidden from me.

"They're here for my protection?"

"Kind of. As long as you do the right thing, you'll be fine. Just don't talk to CNN again."

"CNN? How do you know about CNN?" I'd already had one interview with that news network and was in the process of setting up a second.

"There's bad blood between CNN and the state. Just steer clear, okay?"

The call ended, and I sat on the floor stunned. I felt like I was in a bad spy movie. I didn't know whether I ought to be barricading myself in and sweeping the flat for listening devices or packing Gobi into a bag and climbing down the fire escape. From the way Wendy spoke, it was no big deal, but I found it hard to relax knowing I was being watched so closely.

I sent a message to CNN explaining as vaguely as possible that I had to pull out from the interview. Then I rejected every other interview request from overseas media in my inbox, and I told Lu Xin that I didn't want to speak to any of the Chinese media either. If there was a chance I could say the wrong thing and get myself thrown out of the country—and presumably lose Gobi forever—I wanted to eliminate that risk altogether.

I asked Wendy if she could help find out exactly who the guys in the suits were. I knew it was ridiculous to ask, but I had to know, not for my own safety but for Gobi's. If there was a chance I'd end up being whisked onto the next flight home, I needed to have somewhere to take her.

I spent the rest of the day in the flat. The sun dropped and the room filled with shadows and street lights, but I didn't turn on any of the lights. It felt safer that way.

I ran through possible scenarios, and none of them made me feel any calmer. If someone broke in and tried to take Gobi, I didn't have a clue how to call the police. And if the guys in suits decided to take me, then I would have no choice but to give in and hope that Lu Xin would take good care of Gobi.

I was powerless. Even though the only thing that had changed about the team was Richard's departure, I suddenly felt alone again. I was back to being the one on whose shoulders everything rested, and, for once in my life, I didn't like it. It seemed too much for me to carry.

20

AT SOME POINT IN ALMOST EVERY RACE, I question why I'm running in it. Sometimes it's during those early miles when I'm cold, tired, and just plain grouchy because someone in the tent kept me awake with his snoring. Sometimes it's when my mind drifts to the finish line that's seven or eight hours away. Sometimes it's when I need to take on more water or knock back another salt tablet.

But for every time I ask myself whether running a race is worth all that discomfort, stress, or fear, a moment comes when I know the answer is yes. Sometimes all it takes is to crack out a few more miles and let my body settle into the run. Other times I need to block out thoughts that aren't helpful. And sometimes I need to swallow a salt tablet. In every situation the solution is far simpler than the problem.

On the night before Gobi and I finally left Urumqi, I looked about me and smiled. Even though I had not known any of them two days earlier, I was surrounded by friends. As the laughter got louder and the evening wore on, I knew how grateful I was for the simple way in which their friendships came along at just the right time.

These friendships had started after my second night in the flat. I had spent most of the morning sitting around with Gobi, hoping the door wouldn't burst open and someone rush in to grab either one of us. Eventually Gobi had to get down to ground level and do her business, and we left the flat. As I waited by her favourite bush near the entrance, I watched people going in and out of a restaurant nearby. A guy was manning a barbecue out front, and the smells coming off it were incredible. So, because I'd had enough of eating instant noodles out of a plastic pot in the flat, I decided to take Gobi back up, make sure she was settled, and then come back down and get a quick meal.

That was one of the best decisions I've ever made. I'd eaten Xinjiang barbecue on the last day of the race, but this was even better. The waiter brought over great chunks of perfectly spiced mutton on foot-long metal skewers. I licked the grease from my fingers, sat back, and sighed.

I looked up and noticed a couple of people out on the street staring in at me, grinning from ear to ear. I smiled and waved, then mimed how full I was, and they laughed. It was a fun moment, and soon they came in, bringing a dozen others with them. They all were about my age or a little younger, and they introduced themselves to me, said something about Gobi, and invited me to have a drink and more food with them.

They knew the restaurant staff, and as we tried to communicate in broken English and with translation apps on our phones, they fed me some wickedly spicy noodles, put a shot glass of clear liquid in my hand, and invited me to knock it back with them. Whatever it was, I lost my voice for a few seconds after it went down. A lot more laughter followed, and the night ended with me tripping over the doorstep on the way out, full of great food, a little too much booze, and the sound of new friends' laughter in my ears.

The next night was my last in Urumqi. Kiki had worked wonders and arranged for me and Gobi to fly to Beijing the following day. She'd even flown to Urumqi herself to make sure that everything went smoothly. She knew what a big deal it was, as well as the risks we were facing. Once Gobi was settled and I'd packed what little I'd brought with me, I walked back to the restaurant, hoping to meet my new friends again.

We had another great evening. A couple of shots kicked things off; then before I knew it, the table was filled with skewers and noodles and, eventually, the most amazing cast-iron structure—like the frame of a lampshade but with inch-long spikes sticking out—covered with wonderful-tasting lamb. We laughed about things I can't even remember, talked about nothing much, and when it came time to pay the bill, they insisted I put my cash away.

"Drink tea?" said the one guy who had a few words of English.

I'm more of a coffee guy, but almost two decades of living among the English has taught me to say yes anytime anyone offers tea. Not because I have grown to love the drink but because I know that the offer is actually an invitation to hang out.

So I said yes and followed them all as they walked up the road and walked through a low wooden door set back from the street. I'd assumed we were going to one of their homes, but once inside, it was obvious that this was no home. It looked more like a high-end jewellery store; only instead of display cases filled with rings and necklaces, there were glass-fronted cabinets containing metal tins as big as a pizza and four times as deep.

"I sell tea!" my new friend said. Then, guiding me to a mahogany table that ran almost the entire length of the room, he said, "Sit!"

I watched as he sat in a chair opposite me and arranged an assortment of earth-coloured teapots and delicate bowls, a wooden-handled knife, and a set of mats in front of him. The room fell silent, and everybody watched as his hands glided across his tools, first opening one of the metal tins and then prying a nugget of tea away from the disk inside. He poured water into bowls and swirled it around with all the precision and grace of a magician at a card table. And when, after a few minutes, he poured me a cup of pale amber tea and invited me to drink, I thought I'd never tasted anything quite as wonderful.

More cups of tea followed, all prepared and drunk in almost total silence. The experience wasn't awkward or weird; it was special. I'd never known anything quite like it.

Gradually the chatting and laughter returned. They passed their mobile phones and showed me clips of them dancing around a flat celebrating one of their birthdays. They showed me pictures of them hanging out in a park and of getting dressed up for some big night out. They were fun, and being with them reminded me of the way the search team knew how to laugh with one another. Nobody was trying to be cool, and nobody was trying to exclude other people from the group.

This kind of atmosphere was the exact opposite of what I'd experienced as a teenager in Warwick. Whether it was the tea or the company or the fact that finally, after so long, I was about to get Gobi one giant step closer to home, I started to feel a profound sense of peace about everything.

Eventually it was time to say goodbye. We hugged one another out in front of the shop, and I walked back to my flat holding two beautifully presented bags of tea they had given me. Going up in the lift, I realized they'd paid the bill at the restaurant yet again. They'd never asked me to show them Gobi, even though when I showed them the WeChat group and some of the news coverage about her, their eyes lit up. They didn't want anything from me. They were just offering friendship with no strings attached.

I was nervous about saying goodbye to Gobi at the airport check-in desk, but Kiki had made it clear that there was no way for her to fly with me in the cabin. "Take care down there," I said through the bars of the crate we'd bought. Gobi had an old T-shirt of mine in there with her, and a cushion that was pure luxury. Even so, she knew something odd was happening, I could tell.

For almost all of the three-hour flight, I sat in the cabin fretting about Gobi. Could I trust that she'd made it onto the plane? Enough things had gone wrong already to make me nervous about that possibility. Then there was the experience of being in the hold. I knew she'd cope with the cold—her performance in the Tian Shan mountains proved that she was a rugged little pooch—but how would she manage with all those strange noises? The last time she was locked up was when she was with Nurali, and she had run away from there. I couldn't imagine how stressful she might be finding the experience of being locked up again.

I'd hoped that Gobi was going to take the flight in her stride and waited nervously near the baggage carousel. When her crate was finally wheeled out to me, the sense of relief I felt was so much greater than I imagined it would be. It didn't last. One look and I knew that Gobi had struggled on the flight: she had chewed through her leash, smashed the water bottle, and looked like she had gone ten rounds with a boxer. She had obviously spent the journey feeling petrified, and seeing her in this state made me realize getting all the way to the UK was going to be really stressful for this pup.

Kiki took us straight to her kennels and outlined the plan on the way. Once Gobi had spent thirty days in Kiki's facility, she would be allowed to fly back to England, where she'd spend four months in quarantine. I didn't like the idea of Gobi's spending so much time away from me, but it was by far the best option. I had some work commitments that I needed to get back to, and Kiki promised to send lots of photos and videos of our little girl, keeping me constantly updated about everything. Kiki clearly loved animals, and she seemed to forge an instant bond with Gobi. The feeling was mutual, and I knew they'd both get plenty of cuddles and kisses from each other in the month they would be together.

Even so, saying goodbye to Gobi the next morning was far harder than I anticipated. After all we'd been through, especially in the hotel, I knew she trusted me completely. I'd left her in the hotel or the flat but never for more than an hour or two. She had always greeted me with a massive shower of affection and excitement when I returned. But what would she think when it dawned on her that I wasn't coming back in a few minutes? What would it be like when I finally saw her again, a month down the line, and yet again I'd leave her in an unfamiliar place full of other animals? I feared it might wound her far more deeply than whatever had scarred her head or damaged her hip.

I'd stopped talking to journalists and TV producers almost as soon as I got to the flat, but that didn't mean that I had stopped talking with other people about how Gobi's story could help raise awareness of the importance of looking after abandoned dogs. As well as helping us find a great publisher to work with, Paul de Souza had also introduced us to Jay Kramer, a lawyer who represented some of the biggest writers in the world. Jay knew exactly what he was doing and was helping us think through some of the other ways to share Gobi's story.

Jay and I had been talking for about a week. When he called later that evening, I assumed he wanted to fill me in on his latest conversations with partners. Instead, he had some unexpected—and unwelcome—news.

"Are you making plans for some kind of website?"

"No," I said. I had thought about it vaguely but had done nothing about it. "Why?"

"Someone's just registered at least two domain names that relate to Gobi. They've registered the trademark too."

I was stunned as Jay told me who it was, and I realized I knew the people who were responsible for this. I felt instantly sick and queasy, like I did after I helped Tommy that day. I was struggling to process this new information, and all I could think to say was, "Why?"

"Whoever's done it is trying to cash in. They know that Gobi's been found and that she's coming home, so the story's about to get even bigger."

"But nobody else has ever cared for Gobi. Nobody else owns her."

"Not yet, they don't."

My fears ran deep as though I were in a terrifying nightmare. I thought we'd left all the danger behind us in Urumqi, but was Gobi still at risk? If someone was making a play to claim Gobi on the Internet, wouldn't it make sense for them to try and get Gobi in the flesh? If they had the dog, they could control the story.

Was that why I was being followed by the men in suits and the grey saloon? I'd always thought they were from the government, but was it possible that they were actually reporting to someone else entirely?

These thoughts stayed with me like a mosquito bite. I couldn't stop returning to them long after my call with Jay ended. The more attention I paid them, the more inflamed and painful these dark fears became.

I spent the entire flight home going over the same thoughts. Images of Gobi getting stolen from Kiki's kennels flashed through my mind. Conspiracy theories about what might happen cast deep shadows over me. And a desperate desire to make sure that Gobi was okay left me feeling hollow inside.

Added to that, I was thinking about work.

I had been away from my job for almost two weeks, and I worried that I was pushing the limits of the company's generosity. Everyone had been supportive throughout, and there was never any pressure to return from Urumqi, but I knew my colleagues were working extra hard to cover my workload in my absence. I didn't want to abuse their kindness or take advantage of it.

But I knew that, yet again, I had a choice to make.

I could stick with the plan and leave Gobi in Kiki's care for the next twenty-nine days while we waited for the all-clear on her rabies blood test. I could get on with my work, get back to spending quality time with Lucja, and wait for Gobi to be flown back to the UK, where she'd then spend four months in a secure kennel quarantine. We'd be able to visit her if we wanted, but it was not recommended because the confusion it caused for dogs was frequently traumatic. So if she did ride out the quarantine in the UK, she'd have to do it alone.

The other option was for Gobi to wait the twenty-nine days for the all-clear on the rabies and then spend ninety days living a normal life in Beijing rather than four months locked in a UK facility. With the right tests and paperwork at the end of the ninety days, she could then fly back to the UK without having to set a paw in a quarantine facility.

I knew I could trust Kiki. She had been great right from the very first e-mails we exchanged. But was it fair to leave her the burden of looking after a dog for so long that—just maybe—someone was planning to steal from her? Could I be sure that every single visitor to the kennels would be legit? Could Kiki be asked to maintain that level of vigilance and still run her business at the same time?

I felt guilty leaving Gobi, and if something happened to her again as it did after the first time I said goodbye, I doubted I would have the strength to push through it. I had reached the edges of what I thought I could endure. All I wanted was for these problems to fade away, for the threats to stop, and for Lucja and me to get back to the job of bringing Gobi home.

I knew exactly what I had to do. After hours of thinking it through on my final flight back to the UK, I came up with a plan—the only solution that made any kind of sense.

The trouble was, I had absolutely no idea how I was going to explain it to Lucja or to my boss. They'd think I'd lost it completely.

PART 6

21

SAYING GOODBYE TO LUCJA WAS DIFFICULT. I had been home only a week when, for the second time in less than a month, I bought a last-minute plane ticket and made the twelve-hour journey back to China. I've travelled a lot for work over the years, but this was different. This time I'd be gone for four months.

I'd thought it through, and it all made perfect sense. I needed to go back to Beijing and be with Gobi until her rabies results came through. After that, I figured I might as well stay the following three months so we could live together. The alternative of four months alone in quarantine outside Heathrow Airport simply wasn't an option. I couldn't leave her alone again. A 120-day sentence would turn her into a different dog.

Just like Lucja, my bosses were wholly understanding and supportive. As soon as I returned from Beijing, I phoned and told them I was worried about Gobi, even though we'd finally found her. I mentioned that there were mysterious things going on behind the scenes and that I had to go back to China and spend the duration of the quarantine period with Gobi. I offered to resign, but they refused. Instead, they rushed through approval for a six-month sabbatical. That allowed me to leave the UK knowing I could focus fully on Gobi and have a job to come back to once the dust settled. In the eleven years I'd been working for them, I'd never known of anyone else taking a sabbatical for something like this, and I was staggered by their kindness.

They say it takes a village to raise a child. I think it takes almost half a planet to rescue a dog. At least, that's what it seemed like with Gobi. So many people had helped, from the thousands of supporters who had given money online to the search team who had pounded the streets and gone without sleep in Urumqi. My work colleagues had covered for me, and my bosses had given me generous time off. Kiki and her team had already done much more than I could have asked, and Lucja—who was also surrounded by an army of caring, supportive friends—never once wavered in her unrelenting support of my crazy mission. I could only do what I did because of the help of all those people.

I was looking forward to arriving back in Beijing and seeing Gobi again. I knew Kiki would take great care of her, but in the back of my mind was the thought that anything was possible. At times it seemed as though every other Facebook message I received was yet another warning not to trust anyone and not to let Gobi out of my sight.

Kiki met me at the airport. I climbed into the back of the van to have my face covered in doggie kisses as Gobi scrambled all over me, her tail going a million miles an hour. My reception was just like the night we were reunited back at the Ma family home. Gobi's joy was infectious, and the van was soon full of tears and laughter.

When she had finally calmed down enough for me to speak, I held her in the crook of my arm and said, "I guess this is where you and I start our new life together." She stared back at me, those big eyes locked on mine, just as they had been during the race. My head told me that she couldn't understand what I was saying, but my heart said otherwise. This little dog knew exactly what I meant. And I was convinced that in her own way, she was telling me that whatever the next stage of the adventure held for us, she was all in.

Kiki had found us a place to stay for the first night, but the next day it was time to find a proper home for Gobi and me. With four months to wait until she had passed the strict UK requirements, I wanted to make sure we found a home where she would feel comfortable and safe.

So, like a couple of college graduates who had just moved to a new city, we went looking for a home.

The first place belonged to another pet owner, also one of Kiki's clients. The man was temporarily moving his family back to Mexico and had generously offered to let us stay free of charge while we were in Beijing.

It was a beautiful home in a gated community. High-end cars drove along pristine streets and parked in front of perfectly manicured lawns. The owner and his two dogs welcomed us warmly, and I was pleased to see Gobi trot up and give both the Labradors a friendly sniff and follow them around the den.

"Let me show you the rest of the house," said the owner as he stepped over a low wooden barrier at the bottom of the stairs.

Instinctively I picked up Gobi and lifted her over.

"Oh," he said. "No dogs upstairs. They stay down here."

Oh dear, I thought. "Okay," I said, putting Gobi back down on the other side of the barrier.

Before I'd taken my second step, Gobi was whimpering. By the time I'd gotten halfway up, she had pushed her way through the barrier and was right beside me. I picked her up and followed the guy into an immaculate lounge area that looked as if it was prepped for a *Vogue* photo shoot.

Gobi was straining to get down, her tail shaking wildly. "I don't think this is going to work," I said. "You have such a lovely place. If we stay here, it'll end in tears."

The man smiled back. "I think you're probably right."

Only two months had passed since I first met Gobi, and even though we had been together for only a few days of the race and the week in Urumqi, the bond between us was strong. Now that we had been reunited for the second time, she seemed determined not to let me out of her sight.

The flat we looked at next was everything the previous house was not: it was small, was a little bit shabby, and contained almost no furniture. It was perfect.

I particularly liked the fact that it was up on the eleventh floor. Even though I didn't know how Gobi escaped from Nurali's home, or whether she had been taken, I didn't want to take any chances. After all, it had only taken a few seconds for Gobi to burst through the dog barrier that kept the Labradors out. If she did manage to find a way out of the flat door, surely she wouldn't be able to hack the lift.

Kiki's guys took us to the local Walmart equivalent—WuMart—and we returned to the flat with all the essentials for the next four months: bed linens, a toaster, a frying pan, and a monster bag of dog food.

I don't think I'll ever forget the moment I said goodbye to our helpers and closed the door behind them. I took a moment to look at Gobi, who stared, as she always did at times such as this, right back at me.

"This is it," I said. "Just you and me." I was excited but pretty daunted as well. I knew enough about China to know that I was helpless. I couldn't speak more than four words, and I couldn't read a single character.

If it was possible, Gobi's stare grew even deeper. She tilted her head to one side, trotted back into the flat, jumped up on the couch, curled herself into a ball, gave two heavy sighs, and closed her eyes.

"Fair enough," I said, sitting down beside her. "If you're not stressed, I guess I won't be either."

During the coming days, I got to know Gobi a whole lot better. I knew from the race and our time in Urumqi that she liked to sleep up against me, using me as her pillow, but in Beijing she took being affectionate and tactile to a whole new level.

As soon as I stepped out of the shower the following morning, she was licking my feet and shins as if they were covered in bacon. I just laughed and let her have at it. It was quite a change from the way I'd tried to avoid touching her when I first saw her in the desert. And even though I still didn't have any medical evidence that proved she didn't have rabies, she had charmed her way to my heart. I couldn't resist.

When the rest of me was dry, we went out to explore the local area. I'd seen a few shops at the bottom of the block of flats and a large shopping centre half a mile away. It was a beautiful summer's day with no pollution that I could see, and I fancied a stroll along the nearby canal and a decent cup of coffee.

The walk was easy enough. The coffee, however, was impossible.

I went into the first Starbucks I saw and waited my time in the queue.

I shuffled up to the counter and was just about to give my order when the server looked at Gobi in my arm and pointed to the door.

"No dogs!"

"Oh, it's okay," I said. "I'll just get a takeaway."

"No. Take dog outside." She waved her hands at me as if trying to flick off something unpleasant from her wrists.

I left the store and continued walking. No way was I going to tie Gobi up and leave her outside.

We got pretty much the same reaction at the next coffee place as well as the one after it, where we stopped and sat on the seats out front. I was giving Gobi some water from my hand, just as I did during the race, when a guy came out and told us to leave.

"It's only water!" I said, a bit annoyed by now.

"No!" he shouted. "Must not do. You go."

We walked home more than a little dejected. In a small way I felt that I knew what it was like for Gobi and the countless other stray dogs in China. Being treated like an outcast was no fun at all. Being judged and rejected like that was painful.

If Gobi was bothered by it, she didn't let on. In fact, she seemed happier than ever. She held her head high, and her eyes shone bright as we walked. In many ways it was impossible to tell that she'd been a stray dog on the city streets a couple of weeks earlier, and the deep scar on the top of her head was slowly healing. But the way she carefully held her right hind leg up, avoiding putting weight on it, made it perfectly clear that we needed to fast-track her operation.

Before that, however, I had another task to deal with. One that was even more urgent. I needed to register ownership of Gobi under my name. Chinese law states that every dog owner must carry his licence whenever out in public with his dog. I'd heard that if I was caught without one, Gobi could be taken away that instant.

Kiki helped with the paperwork, and once it was done and I slipped the dog licence into my wallet, I felt a huge weight lift from my shoulders. Not only was I now legal, but I also had another line of defense against someone else trying to claim ownership of Gobi.

The more time I spent with Gobi, the more I learned about her. The more I learned about her, the more intrigued and amazed by her I became.

Every time we walked past a piece of rubbish on the pavement, she'd pull at the lead and drag me over to let her scavenge for food. It told me that her street days in Urumqi probably weren't her only experience of having to fend for herself, and I'd often watch her devour the leftover remnants inside a takeaway wrapper and wonder just how many secrets her life held.

In spite of being a connoisseur of street food, she had already shown me in Urumqi that she could adapt easily to a more sophisticated style of life. I guess not every dog is suited to flat living, but Gobi settled into it with ease. In many ways she never seemed happier than when she was curled up beside me, staring deep into my eyes as we hung out on the couch. She didn't bark when I was with her, she didn't attack what little furniture we had, and on the few occasions when she didn't manage to hold on until we'd got outside to do her business, I could see she felt guilty about it.

The first time Gobi had an accident was soon after we moved in. I'd decided to get my coffee fix in the flat that morning, and I didn't quite read her signs correctly. I thought Gobi was spinning around and sniffing the door because she'd heard a dog barking in a nearby flat.

It was only when she disappeared into the bathroom for a minute and re-emerged, head down, walking sideways up to me, that I knew something was wrong. With her ears pinned down and head hung low, she wore a look of complete shame.

I checked the bathroom and found a small lake of dog pee on the floor. Poor thing. I apologized profusely, and as soon as I'd cleaned up, I took her downstairs to her preferred toilet stop in the bushes near the entrance.

The only thing Gobi didn't like was being left alone in the flat. I tried to leave her as little as possible, but there were times when I had no other choice. If I needed to go to the gym to run on the treadmill, or if we were out of food and I needed to go to the supermarket, she had to stay back. Almost every time we did go out together, we would be spotted at least once or twice and asked for a photo. Gobi's story had been a huge hit all over China, and leaving her tied up outside a supermarket or Starbucks while I went inside wasn't a risk I was prepared to take.

But leaving her was hard. I'd try to slip out the door as quickly as I could, often having to gently block her from following me. I'd always check and double-check that the door was locked, and as I walked away, I could hear her making the same noise that she did at the river crossing. That pained, high-pitched whimpering sound cut through me every time.

As tough as it was to leave her, whenever I returned, she was just as overjoyed as she had been at the Ma family house the night we were reunited. She'd spin and sprint and yelp with pure adrenaline-rush excitement. Eventually she'd calm down enough for me to pick her up, and a deep sense of calm would fall over her, again just like at the river crossing. It's still the same today; whenever Gobi is in my arms, I'm convinced that she doesn't have a care in the world.

To be trusted so much by a living creature is a powerful thing, especially when you know it could choose to leave at any time. But Gobi never showed any signs of wanting to be anywhere other than right by my side.

Every morning I'd wake up to her staring at me, her head so close to mine that I could feel her breath on my cheek. Most days, if I didn't start playing with her soon enough, she'd start licking my face. That was one sign of doggie affection that I didn't find quite so cute back in the early days, and it got me straight out of bed.

We'd get downstairs quickly so she could do her business, but it was always obvious to me that what Gobi wanted more than anything was to get back up to the flat and settle down for a good cuddle.

For me to be on the receiving end of that kind of love and devotion is a special thing. To be able to care for her, to be able to give her the kind of attention and affection she needs, touches something deep down in my heart.

Love. Devotion. Attention. Affection. In many ways I feel they all disappeared from my life when I hit ten. A whole decade would pass before I met Lucja and felt all that good stuff begin to flood back into my life.

What Gobi introduced to my life was the chance for me to treat someone young and vulnerable in the way I wanted to be treated when my life was shaken out of control. Gobi needed me. Even though I'm still not sure I can adequately put words to the feelings, I know that rescuing her has healed wounds I didn't know were within me.

Not that it was perfect. The TV, for example, was terrible.

I expected there to be at least a basic range of channels. Maybe a little BBC or some Fox News from time to time. No chance. All I could get were two channels: a Chinese news service that looped an hour-long summary of the previous day's events and a movie channel with the occasional Hollywood offering presented with Chinese subtitles. I got my hopes up when I discovered this second one, but it turned out that most of your favourite B-list movie stars have an awfully long catalogue of films that are so bad they've never made it to our Western screens. I watched some truly terrible movies in those early days. I eventually got bored and gave up trying. I was fed up with nothing to do.

The Internet was a problem too. It took me a week to work out how to get around the extensive filters the Chinese authorities put on the web, but my hack made streaming any video content almost impossible.

Gobi and I tried to spend more time outside. The mile-long footpath along the canal was always a good place to walk, especially when the construction workers were on their breaks. They ignored us as they gathered around the food vendors on the street, who had a great trade going among them. Gobi and I soon learned that the best stalls of all were the ones serving jianbing—what I called a Beijing burrito. Think of a thin crepe with an egg cooked inside it and a load of crushed, crispy fried wonton, delicious spices, and chilli. Gobi and I couldn't get enough of those.

We had got thrown out of almost all of the coffee shops we

tried, but, thankfully, we found a Starbucks that was happy to break the rules and let us sit outside. Best of all was a little independent café where the staff not only allowed us inside but even ignored me when I put Gobi on the seat and fed her a bit of my pastry.

For a city that doesn't allow dogs in taxis or buses, and has only recently passed a law allowing guide dogs to travel on subways, this was a major success. We made sure we supported them well throughout our stay.

As fun as it was to learn about this new life together, one thing continually worried me—Gobi's damaged hip. She did her best to hide it and had learned how to skip along without putting too much weight on it. But if I ever picked her up the wrong way or tried to hold her on my left side instead of my right, she'd let out a little cry of pain.

In addition, the injury on her head hadn't healed as well as Kiki or I had hoped.

So after a week in the flat, I broke the bad news to Gobi.

"No café for you and me today, little one. We're going to see the vet."

22

I COULDN'T STAND THE NOISE. I STOOD IN THE corridor and tried to block out the sound of Gobi gripped by pain and fear, but it was no use. Those squeals and cries were the most horrible noise I'd ever heard in my whole life.

I'd read somewhere that to prevent dogs from associating deep pain and fear with their owners, you shouldn't be in the same room with them when they're given an injection. Even without that advice, I don't think I would have been able to be by her side.

When the anaesthetic kicked in and she finally grew quiet, one of the nurses came and found me.

"She's fine. Do you want to come in?"

Thanks to Kiki, Gobi was about to be operated on in one of the top veterinary hospitals in the city. And thanks to the Chinese media, all of the nurses and doctors had already heard of Gobi. That (plus a good word from Kiki) meant Gobi had the most experienced surgical team and both Kiki and I were allowed to wash up, put on the blue scrubs, and join the team in the operating theatre.

After numerous scans and extensive consultations, the staff unanimously confirmed what I'd been told in Urumqi—that the cause of Gobi's pain and strange hopping was an injury to her right hip. Whether she had been hit by a car or a human, it was impossible to say, but sometime during her runabout in Urumqi, she'd picked up the injury, which had forced her hip out of the pelvis.

The staff recommended Gobi have a femoral head ostectomy: a form of hip surgery where the top of the femur is removed but not replaced with anything, leaving the body to heal itself and the joint to reform with scar tissue.

I'd been reassured a dozen times that this was a standard procedure that could yield excellent results. I was confident in the team and felt we were in safe hands. But as I stood and watched them about to begin the hour-long operation, I was still a nervous wreck.

Again, it was the noises that got me, though this time Gobi was too heavily drugged to make a sound. She was lying with her tongue hanging out like an old sock, breathing steadily into the mask placed over her mouth, while the nurses shaved away all the fur from her right hip. What bothered me this time was the sound of the machines that were monitoring her heart rate and oxygen levels. Ever since Garry's death, I have always hated hearing the sound of those machines on TV. They remind me of the night I stood in my sister's room and listened to the medics try to save him, and whenever I hear the steady beeps, I ask myself the same, simple question: *If I'd got out of bed sooner, would I have been able to save him?*

A conversation broke out among the doctors, their voices slightly raised. Kiki must have sensed my concern because she tapped me on the shoulder and spoke softly. She told me they were trying to decide how much of the drug to give her to prevent a heart attack without going too far and inducing one.

"I hope they know what they're doing," I muttered. I felt physically sick inside.

Eventually, when the room quietened down and they started to operate, I told Kiki I had to go. "Come and get me as soon as it's all done," I said. "I can't be in here."

The hour felt more like a month, but when it was finally over, the head surgeon came to reassure me that the surgery had gone well and Gobi would soon be coming around. I sat beside her in the recovery room and watched her gradually wake up.

There was a moment when she looked at me, and everything was just as it was every morning, her big eyes locked on mine. But a second later the pain must have kicked in, for her high-pitched whimpering started up again. Looking at her, listening to her, I understood clearly that she was in a world of pain. Nothing I could do seemed to help.

Within less than a day, Gobi's true spirit was shining through again. She was in pain from the operation, and I knew her hip would take weeks to fully repair itself, but by the time I got her back to the flat, she was back to her old tail-wagging, face-licking self.

I, on the other hand, was feeling unsettled. I couldn't be sure whether it was seeing Gobi in pain that had bothered me or the memories of Garry's death, but I knew for certain that in the days and weeks that followed, I was still worried about Gobi's safety.

Right from the start of our time in Beijing, I'd felt a little nervous about the number of people who recognized Gobi. But as we spent more and more time in the flat during her recovery, I grew a little paranoid. If I was down in the lobby waiting for a lift and someone else joined me—especially if the person wasn't Chinese—I'd make a point of getting out at either the tenth or the twelfth floor and using the stairs to reach the eleventh, looking over my shoulder as I went. I knew it was silly, and I knew that if someone did want to snatch Gobi, it would take a lot more than my amateur spy impression to keep us safe. But the instinct to be suspicious about strangers was too strong to resist.

It didn't help that the rest of the flats on my floor were also short-term rentals. That meant there was a constant turnover of people. Remembering the visit from the guys in suits in Urumqi, I eyed all residents carefully.

"It's okay to go out and live a normal life," said Kiki after I shared my fears one day.

A normal life? I wasn't even sure I knew what that meant anymore. Four months earlier I'd been working sixty-hour weeks, away three nights out of seven, fitting in my training at nine or ten at night while others were watching TV. I was filling my time with work, training, and trying to live life with Lucja in our home in Edinburgh. Now I was on long-term leave, living thousands of miles away, barely running, trying to keep safe a little dog who seemed at times to be the most famous pup in the whole world. Normal was a lifetime away.

I was also concerned about the number of photo requests Gobi got whenever we went out. Most people were great, and I liked that Gobi made people happy, but I knew, for some, she was just a cute photo opportunity.

Part of the stray dog problem in China stems from people's buying pedigree dogs, bringing them back to their flats, and then getting annoyed when the dogs make a mess on the floor or trash the furniture. In a country where there's so much wealth, dogs are sometimes treated as a fashion accessory—temporary and disposable.

Gobi deserved better than that.

A month into my stay in Beijing, the result of the rabies test was due.

All throughout the twenty-nine days we'd spent waiting, my instincts had told me Gobi would be fine. I knew the test would come back clear and we could move on to the next phase of waiting the ninety days for the second round of tests. But as much as I believed this, a part of me had started to wonder. What if Gobi did have rabies after all? What then? If we couldn't bring Gobi back to the UK, would we move to China to live together? Instead of bringing Gobi home, would we have to bring home to Gobi?

The result was as we expected. Gobi didn't have rabies. I exhaled a huge sigh of relief, cheered with Lucja, and shared the news with the rest of the world via our growing social media accounts. The reaction brought a tear to my eye.

So many strangers were heavily invested in Gobi's story, and it still amazes me to read of the ways in which she has touched people's lives. For instance, one woman who has cancer told me that she looks at our Facebook, Twitter, and Instagram pages every day to see what Gobi and I are up to. "I've been with you from the start," she told me.

I love that the story isn't just about Gobi and me trying to get home. Whether people have lost their jobs, are suffering with depression, or are going through marriage troubles, this little dog has put a smile on so many people's faces.

In the end, it was the running that helped ease my fears. Soon after Gobi's operation, I was invited by someone I'd met in Urumqi to take part in a single-stage race in a different part of the Gobi Desert. The organizers had gathered fifty of the world's best sixty-mile specialists for the race in Gansu Province, next to Xinjiang. It's not a distance I usually run—at least, not as a one-day, point-to-point race—but somehow I was still in pretty good shape from the training I'd managed to put in for the Atacama race I'd skipped.

But now the Gansu race organizers were offering free lodging and free return flights home to Edinburgh in exchange for my taking part in the sixty-mile run and giving them a PR boost by meeting with journalists. I had quite a few requests for interviews and photo shoots, all of them from journalists interested in getting an update on Gobi and capturing me in action. The thought of being able to use the ticket to fly back and see Lucja again was too tempting to resist.

Just four days before the race, I received even better news from the race organizers. They had a few spaces still available and were willing to pay to fly in any other elite runners who might want to compete. I called Lucja right away. It was a crazy idea to come all the way to China and run so far at such short notice, especially as six weeks earlier she'd completed a brutal five-day, 300-mile challenge across Holland. But as well as being a world-class runner, who finished thirteenth among the women in the 2016 Marathon des Sables, Lucja's a tough lady who loves an adventure. She said yes immediately. Forty-eight hours later she was on a plane heading east.

I was a little worried about Gobi. But Kiki had promised to take good care of her, and I could trust her. Besides, I had the feeling that Gobi wouldn't mind a few days of serious pampering in Kiki's recovery pool and grooming parlour.

As soon as I knew Lucja was coming, I was all in. Running has played a special part in our relationship, and the race coincided with our eleventh wedding anniversary. I couldn't think of a better way to celebrate how far we'd come together.

One of my favourite memories of running with Lucja comes from the first Marathon des Sables we competed in together. As with most multi-stage ultras, you get your finisher's medal at the end of the long stage (usually the penultimate stage of the race). I was surprised how well I was doing, and as the long stage came to a close, I knew I had secured my finisher's spot just outside the top one hundred. For a first-time runner—who almost quit on day one—among thirteen hundred other runners, it wasn't too bad a result.

I cleared the final ridge that hid the finish line from view and saw the crowds up ahead, cheering the runners home. And there, a few hundred feet back from the finish, was Lucja. She'd started earlier than me that day, and I hadn't expected to see her on the course. But there she was, her hand shielding her eyes from the sun as she looked back in my direction.

"What are you doing here?" I said when I finally reached her. "I thought you'd have finished an hour ago."

"I could have," she said. "But I wanted to finish with you, so I waited."

We crossed the line hand in hand. She could have finished so much higher up, but she chose to wait for me.

I still think about that when I run today.

It was good to get back to the desert, good to be able to run without traffic or pollution, and most of all, great to see Lucja. We'd been apart for almost six weeks, and I wanted to spend every minute I could with her. So even though I thought I could have placed fairly well, I was far happier to hang back and run the race together with her.

The route led us twice around a thirty-mile loop. It was a hot day, easily in the 110s, and as we completed the first lap, we saw that the medical tent was already doing good business. And a bunch of people had decided to throw in the towel and quit. They had started the race far too quickly, had pushed too hard, had struggled in the conditions, and didn't want to keep pushing through a second loop. I've bailed on more than my fair share of training runs, though never because of the heat. It's the Scottish mud, wind, and rain that send me back to the car.

We ran the first thirty miles a bit slower than I'd planned, but I figured we still had a good eight hours to get around the rest of the course before the fourteen-hour cut-off.

As we started the second loop, Lucja had second thoughts.

"You go, Dion. I don't have it in me," she said.

Lucja and I have run enough races to know when it's time to throw in the towel and when it's time to grit it out. I took a long look at her. She was tired, but she was still fighting. This was no time for towels.

"We can do this," I said. "I've got a television crew following me, and the organizers have really looked after us; we owe it to them. I'll get you round it. Just stick with me."

She did what she does so well and dug in. We kept going, running from marker to marker, ticking the miles off as we went.

Things got worse, with eighteen miles to go, when a sandstorm struck up. Visibility was cut to less than one hundred feet, and it was getting hard to see the markers. I thought back to the huge sandstorm at the end of the long day when Tommy nearly died. I didn't have Gobi to look after, but I had Lucja to protect. With no sign of any race officials around us, I started to formulate an emergency plan if the sandstorm got any worse or if Lucja started to tank.

She didn't, and the storm eventually lifted, but the winds were still strong. They had blown our hats off, and our eyes stung with sand. Debris was flying everywhere. We pushed on, though we were making slow progress between markers, only moving on to the next one if and when we could see it. Lucja tried taking a gel to give her some energy, but every time she did, she threw it back up again.

When we reached the next checkpoint, it was a mess, everything blown away and the volunteers looking shell-shocked. We pressed on, though, despite the fact that we were running slower than ever. I thought it was odd that nobody was passing us, but I put all my effort into encouraging Lucja to block out the pain and keep going.

We passed another half-destroyed checkpoint and kept going, knowing that we had eight miles left to run.

It was dark by now, and when a car approached with its headlights on full, the whole sky lit up. "What are you doing?" the driver asked.

"We're racing," I said, too tired to try and be funny.

"But a lot of people have been pulled already because of the sandstorm."

"Nobody told us at the checkpoint. We've only a few miles left, and we're not stopping now."

"Okay then," he said, before driving off.

Those last few miles were some of the hardest I've ever seen Lucja complete. Amid tears, shouts, and serious pain, she held on to an unshakable determination to finish.

As we crossed the line, I held her hand.

"Happy anniversary," I said. "I'm so proud of you."

We got to spend one night together back in Beijing before Lucja had to fly home for work. Kiki met us outside the airport, and yet again Gobi was a hurricane of excitement in the back of the van. This time, though, it wasn't just me she was licking. Gobi seemed to know instantly that Lucja was special and gave her the full welcoming experience.

Gobi showed Lucja her affection all night. I crashed soon after we made it back to the flat, but Lucja didn't get any sleep at all because Gobi decided that an even longer bonding session was required. By the time I woke up, they were inseparable.

I made some big decisions after the race.

First, I decided I was going to say no to all interview requests for the rest of my time in Beijing. Some journalists had contacted me during the race, telling me they needed to get a photo of Gobi and asking if they could visit her at Kiki's place while I was out of town. They'd even gone to the point of directly contacting Kiki, who of course said no. I didn't like this, as I'd tried hard to keep our location secret.

Being with Lucja had made me think about what life might be like when Gobi and I finally got home. I was sure there would be some press interest for a week or two, but I knew I'd want life to return to normal as quickly as possible—whatever the new normal would look like. So I made the choice to stop doing interviews. It was time for Gobi and me to go dark.

The second decision I made was about running.

The sixty-miler had been a piece of cake. I looked at the times of the different finishers and worked out that I could have made it into the top ten—not a bad possible result given that the elite field included some 2:05 marathon runners from Kenya. A couple of weeks later I had a conversation with the organizers of an upcoming 104-mile ultra-race, the Mt Gaoligong Ultra. As part of the invitation to run, we talked about my doing a few interviews with UK running magazines. The opportunity to travel to another part of China, to the city of Tengchong in Yunnan Province, close to Myanmar, was a great drawcard for me. I'd never done a non-stop hundred-miler before, so I certainly wasn't signing up to compete with the idea of winning.

It was a brutal race in the mountains. Climbing 29,000 feet altogether, I was pushed to my limits and was close to pulling out at one point during the race. My fitness wasn't as good as it should have been, but seeing the finish line after thirty-two-non-stop hours, I was stoked to complete it. I received my medal—styled in the form of a sheep bell to remind runners of the local herders we ran past in the mountains—finishing a respectable fourteenth out of fifty-seven hard-core endurance athletes.

23

ONE DAY GOBI AND I WERE SHIVERING, TRYING to wrap up against the winter wind that whipped through the ageing flat windows; the next we were unable to sleep, fighting for air as the sweltering heat sapped the life out of us.

15 November was the day the government turned on the heat nationwide. It was the start of our toughest times in Beijing.

Almost as soon as the heating went on, the pollution increased. Like everyone in Beijing, I'd learned to monitor the air quality and tailor my day accordingly. If the index was below 100, I'd take Gobi out without any worry at all. Above 200, and I'd keep our walks short. Above 400, and even the fifty-foot walk from the bottom of the block of flats to my favourite Japanese restaurant was enough to leave my eyes stinging.

I'd heard that when the levels are between 100 and 200 and you're outside, it's like smoking a pack of cigarettes a day. Two hundred is two packs, 300 is three, and anything above that is like a whole carton.

With the coal-fired power stations spewing their heavy smoke, the sky was so full of toxic filth that you didn't dare open the windows in the flat.

Trying to avoid the pollution led to a sense that our freedom had been cut. We were not able to go for walks or out for coffee. Everything stopped. We felt as though we'd been cut off from the world.

The change was not good for Gobi. After just a few days of shutting ourselves away in the flat, I could tell she was struggling. She stopped eating, barely drank anything, and lay about with the saddest look on her face I had ever seen. About the only thing I could do to get her up and moving was to take her out into the corridor and throw a tennis ball for her to chase and bring back. It was the kind of game she would have played for hours had we been out by the canal, but up in the flat block, with the security lights continually switching themselves off and plunging us into darkness, she'd want to play for only thirty minutes.

Thinking the problem with the corridor might be too many distracting smells wafting out from under our neighbours' doors, I took Gobi down to the basement car park one day. I knew it was usually empty during the day, so there would be plenty of space for her to run and chase the ball, just like she used to.

As soon as the lift doors opened on the cavernous car park, Gobi planted her feet as if she were a hundred-year-old oak tree and refused to move.

"Really?" I said. "You're definitely not going in?"

She stared ahead into the darkness. She would not be moved.

On the night that I came back from my evening sushi and she didn't get up to greet me, I knew we were in trouble.

The next day the vet took a good look at her and diagnosed

kennel cough. The remedy was a course of medication and a week locked up in the flat.

With Lucja not due to come back to Beijing until Christmas, no media duties to fulfil, and no way of getting out, the days dragged by. Twice each day we'd take the tennis ball out to the corridor, and every evening I'd squint my eyes up tight against the pollution and hurry over to the Japanese restaurant. The flat was a furnace, but I dared not open the windows and let more pollution in. So every morning I'd wake up feeling hungover, regardless of whether I'd drunk three beers the night before or none at all.

I'd go to the gym from time to time, but I could stream only an hour's worth of video before my Internet account dropped out. Without a screen to distract me, I'd soon lose interest.

I tried to work on my strength and conditioning in the flat, but it was hopeless. The pollution was everywhere. Even though I washed the floor and wiped the surfaces regularly, every time I did push-ups, my hands would be covered in black grime, which must have crept in through invisible cracks in the windows.

Just as I was starting to slip into the darkness, Gobi recovered. Her timing was perfect. I'd wake up to see her staring at me, I'd receive the customary lick, and my day would be off to the best of starts. How could I be depressed when I had Gobi all to myself?

Gobi grew in confidence every day. Once she bounced back from the kennel cough, her old self re-emerged. Even when we were going outside so she could do her business, she'd walk with her head up, her feet light, and her eyes bright. I loved seeing her look so confident and self-assured.

Yet again Gobi got me through. I thought about how she had put herself through so much, from the run to the time on the streets in Urumqi, just so she could find a forever home with people who would love and care for her. If she could tough it out, then so could I.

During those long days, I had a lot of time to think and a lot of things to think about.

I thought about coming home and how, even though I compete wearing the Aussie flag and would never support any sporting nation other than Australia, the UK is now my home. I've lived here for fifteen years and seen so many of the good things in my life flourish here. My running, my career, my marriage—all these things have taken off in the UK. I couldn't think of anywhere else I'd rather take Gobi back to.

I thought about my dad too. I was in my early twenties when my real father made contact and came into my life. Things were complicated, and it wasn't possible for us to have a lasting relationship.

Even though I never had that father–son experience that many of my friends have, I am grateful to him for one thing. He was born in Birmingham, England, but as a child his family emigrated to Australia. My dad didn't give me any money, and he didn't give me any support when I needed it most. But when I was an adult and ready to make a fresh start thousands of miles away from home, my dad's nationality meant that I was eligible for a UK passport.

I thought about my mum too. Around the same time my dad reappeared in my life, my mum became sick. She phoned me one day before Lucja and I met. I was surprised to hear her voice, given that we'd spoken only on Christmas Day in the years before that.

When she told me that she was seriously ill, I was stunned.

As I watched her go through treatment and saw her get dangerously close to death, it pulled us closer. She wanted to make things better, and that was exactly what we vowed to do. We built the relationship back up from there. We took our steps slowly, but over the years we've at least grown to become friends.

Waiting around in the flat, counting down the days until I'd see Lucja again, I also thought about why finding Gobi had been so significant for me. It wasn't hard to figure it out.

It was about keeping my promise.

I'd vowed to bring Gobi back, no matter what it took. Finding her, keeping her safe, and making it possible to fly back home meant that I had kept my word. After all the ups and downs, I'd been able to rescue her. I'd given her the safety and security I had been so desperate for when my life went wrong as a kid.

The day Gobi stood by my side and looked up from my yellow gaiters and stared into my eyes, she had a look about her that I'd never seen. She trusted me from the outset. She even put her life in my hands. To have a complete stranger do that to you, even if it is a four-legged stray, is a powerful, powerful thing.

Did Gobi save me? I don't think I was lost, but I know for sure that she has changed me. I've become more patient, and I've had to deal with the demons of the past. She has added to the good things in my life that started when Lucja and I met and then continued when I discovered running. Maybe I'll no longer feel the need to run long-distance races to sort out the problems from my past. In many ways, by finding Gobi, I've found more of myself.

When Christmas was finally a few days away and I stood in the airport and watched Lucja walk through the arrival door, I couldn't help crying. It was just like the day she waited for me at the Marathon des Sables: the longest, toughest, most gruelling part of the challenge was behind us. We'd made it. Soon we'd be going home.

24

SOMETIMES, IF I CLOSE MY EYES AND CONCENTRATE hard enough, I can remember all the times I've been told that I was going to fail. I still can picture my junior high school headmaster holding out his hand for me to shake, a fake smile stuck on his face as he whispered that one day I'd end up in prison.

I can see countless sports coaches, teachers, and parents of people I thought were my friends, all looking at me with disapproval or disappointment, telling me that I'd wasted whatever talent I had and was nothing but a bad influence.

I remember my mum at the lowest points of her grief and how helpless I felt.

For a long time I tried to block out those memories. I got pretty good at it. I needed to, for whenever I let down my guard and gave those dark memories some room to move, I instantly regretted it.

Like the very first time I ran an ultra-marathon. I was nervous right from the start, but as the miles inched by and the hours stretched out, I started to doubt myself.

Who am I to line up alongside all these other runners who know what they were doing?

What was I thinking, to try and run thirty miles with barely any training?

Was I really a fool to think that I could do it?

As these grew louder within me, the answers soon came.

You're nothing.

You're no good.

You're never going to finish.

Four miles from the finish, I proved those voices right. I quit.

This was a few weeks before my first multi-stage ultra, the 155-mile Kalahari race that Lucja had first spotted in the book I'd bought for her previous birthday. In the days after I bailed on my first ever ultra-marathon, the doubting voices within me grew louder and louder. When friends asked whether I really thought I was capable of running so far, given that I'd not managed a measly thirty-miler, I was almost convinced they were right.

Who am I to think I could do it?

I'm nothing.

I'm no good.

I'm never going to succeed.

But something happened between bailing on the thirty and starting the Kalahari. I wish I could say that I had a flash of light or a great training sequence, like in my all-time favourite movie, *Rocky*.

I didn't.

I just decided to try my best to ignore the voices that told me I was a failure.

Whenever those toxic whispers started up within me, I chose to tell myself a better story.

I can do it.
I'm not a failure.
I'm going to prove everyone wrong.

Our flight out of Beijing was late on New Year's Eve. I spent the day cleaning the flat, walking Gobi, and saying goodbye to the guys in the Japanese restaurant who had served up kimchi hot pot, sushi, salad, and friendship on an almost daily basis. They even gave me a bottle of the secret salad dressing that I had come to crave.

As we waited for Kiki to pick us up at the flat that evening, Gobi knew something was up. She was wired about as tight as I'd ever seen her, sprinting around the empty flat. When we finally walked out of the block of flats for the last time ever, Gobi raced towards Kiki's car as if it was made out of bacon.

I was a little calmer.

I sat and watched the street lights pass by, thinking about the people and places that had become important to us during the four months and four days we had spent in Beijing.

We passed the hotel gym where I had tried so hard to keep up my training. I thought back to all those times when the Internet had dropped out and I had to quit after just one hour on the treadmill. I'd found the whole thing frustrating but nothing more. A mark of how much had changed in my life was that I'd been able to let go of it so easily.

There was the Little Adoption Shop, where Chris worked, and where we donated £10,000 from the donations left over from the Bring Gobi Home fund. Without Chris and his careful advice to Lu Xin about how to conduct the search for Gobi, I knew we never would have found her. Without Chris, who knew where Gobi would be by now?

I thought about all the other people I'd met in Beijing, as well as those back in Urumqi. It was hard to leave so many great people behind, especially since my time in China had completely changed my view on the country and its people.

If I'm honest, when I arrived in China for the Gobi race, my view of the Chinese was a bit clichéd. I thought they were closed-off and serious, rude and uncaring. In that first journey from Urumqi to the race start, I saw in the people only what I expected to see. No wonder I didn't think much of the place.

But everything that happened with Gobi changed my perspective. Now I know the Chinese are lovely, genuine, hospitable people. Once they let you into their hearts and homes, they're incredibly generous and unfailingly kind. One family I'd never met but who had followed the story loaned me a £1,000 electric bike for the duration of my stay. They didn't ask for anything in return, not even a selfie with Gobi.

People were the same in Urumqi. The city itself might be full of closed-circuit TV cameras and security guards outside public parks, but the people are some of the friendliest, most generous, and most kind-hearted I've ever met. I'm pleased to have a connection with them and know that it won't be long before I return.

And then there's Kiki. She agreed to help us when everybody else was saying no. She came to Urumqi to make sure Gobi got out safely, and she spent the whole four months that we were in Beijing in a state of nervous tension, feeling responsible not just for Gobi's well-being but also for my welfare. I called her 24/7 with all sorts of questions (How do I pay for more electricity? Gobi's not feeling well. What do I do? Where do I go to buy pollution masks?). She was never too busy or too tired to help, and she never once complained when I asked if she could take Gobi for a few days while I went out of town. She even sent video updates every couple of hours to me, and I was kept fully up-to-date with all the ways her staff pampered Gobi. Kiki made her team available to me as well. Her drivers ferried us everywhere, dropped off supplies to me in the flat, took care of the paperwork, and tended to countless details. They did more than I could have ever asked.

We pulled up outside the airport, unloaded the bags, and let Gobi take one last potty break before zipping her into the special doggie carrier that she'd be in for most of the journey.

UK law prohibits dogs from being in the cabin for any flights, in or out of the country. After she'd been so traumatized by travelling in the cargo hold when we left Urumqi, I vowed never to stow her away down there again. That meant our journey home was going to be long and complicated: a ten-hour flight to Paris, a five-hour drive to Amsterdam, a twelve-hour overnight ferry crossing to Newcastle in northern England, and a two-and-a-half-hour drive back home to Edinburgh. With all the waiting around added on, the whole thing was going to take forty-one hours.

We'd purposely paid extra for business class to make sure Gobi was comfortable and able to be next to me in the cabin. I felt pretty good as I walked up to the counter and was seen straightaway. I handed over my passport to the woman at the desk, stepped back, and thought about how much life had changed for Gobi. Six months earlier she'd been living on the edge of the Gobi Desert, desperate enough for survival to run three marathons alongside a total stranger. Now she was about to fly business class to the chic city of Paris, of all places.

I was pulled out of my daydream by the sound of Kiki having an increasingly loud conversation with the Chinese check-in lady. During my time in China, I'd come to understand that anytime the volume rises in a conversation, trouble is brewing. I closed my eyes, listening as whatever issue Kiki had encountered grew bigger and bigger.

"What's going on, Kiki?"

"Did you book Gobi on to the flight?"

It was as if all the air around me suddenly turned stale.

"I didn't do it," I said. "I thought you were doing it."

Kiki shook her head. "Lucja supposed to do it."

Kiki turned back to the clerk, and the conversation continued. I dialled Lucja.

"Did you book Gobi on?"

"No," she said. "Kiki was supposed to do it."

It was obvious that this was just a simple misunderstanding between the two of them. They'd both been so busy organizing so much from other ends of the world that this little detail had been missed. And I was sure it was going to be relatively simple to fix. Maybe a little expensive but simple enough.

"Kiki," I said, tapping her on the shoulder. "Just get them to tell me how much it's going to cost, and we can get on with it."

She shook her head. "She say she can't. No way to put Gobi on system now. It's impossible."

I closed my eyes and tried to take control of my breathing. Steady in, steady out. Keep calm, Dion. Keep calm.

Another check-in clerk came over and joined the conversation, pushing the volume up another couple of levels. By now Kiki was in full flow, pointing at Gobi and me in turn. I could do nothing but stand there and panic in silence.

All the paperwork we had to allow Gobi into the UK was tailored to our journey. That meant that if we arrived at Newcastle any later than midnight on 2 January, it would all be invalid, and I'd have to get Gobi seen and signed off by another vet. At the very best, that would add another day or two to the journey. At worst, it could take another week.

A third official joined the two behind the desk, and as he did, the atmosphere changed. The volume dropped, and he listened while Kiki talked.

After a few words from the boss, Kiki turned to me. "Gobi not booked on this flight," she said. I knew what was coming next, how we would have to book her onto the next flight out, but that would cost us an extra—

"Go to that counter there," Kiki said, pointing to another Air France desk nearby, "pay two hundred pounds, and he say they will get her on board."

I was stunned. "On board *this* flight?"

"Yes."

I didn't waste any time. I paid the fee at the other counter and came back to get my boarding pass.

"I told them Gobi a famous dog," said Kiki, and she smiled as I waited. "They know story and wanted to make it happen for you."

As soon as I had my passport and my boarding pass in my pocket, it was Gobi selfies and smiles all around for the check-in staff.

I finally said goodbye to Kiki at passport control, then drifted through security, exhaling a ton of stress as I went.

"Wait one moment," said a woman as I started putting my shoes back on. "You go with him."

I looked up to see a serious-looking man staring at me from the side of the scanners. I grabbed Gobi—still in her carry-on bag—and my luggage and followed him down a narrow corridor. He showed me into a sparse, windowless room that had nothing much more than a desk, two chairs, and a large bin full of confiscated lighters and water bottles.

Keep calm, Dion. Keep calm.

The guy stared at my passport and boarding pass and started typing at the computer. Minutes passed, and still he didn't speak. I wondered what it was that I'd done or said that could have landed me in trouble. I knew I hadn't outstayed my visa, and it had been weeks since I'd last given an interview. Could it be the pills that Lucja had given me to help keep Gobi calm during the flight?

More typing. More silence. Then, suddenly, he spoke. "We check dog."

My heart sank. I knew two hundred was far too cheap a price to pay to sort things out. And I knew that by now Kiki would be gone, and even though I had a file stuffed with paperwork from the vet, including proof that Gobi's vaccinations were up-to-date and that she'd passed the ninety-day assessment required before she could be brought into the UK, I'd have absolutely no chance of explaining anything to anyone. Without Kiki, I'd be at the mercy of Chinese bureaucracy.

The guy stopped typing, picked up the phone, and spoke for a moment.

"You wait minute," he said, once he had hung up and turned back to his keyboard.

Gobi was still in her bag, which I was clutching on my lap.

Through the mesh I could see her looking up at me. I wanted to tell her that it was going to be okay, to get her out and give her a cuddle to reassure her—as well as myself—but doing so wasn't worth the risk.

So I waited. It was the longest minute of my life.

The phone rang. I listened to one half of the conversation, clueless about what was being said or what the outcome might be.

"Okay," he said eventually. "Dog cleared to fly. You go."

"Where?" I asked.

"Fly."

I hurried back down the corridor, past the scanning machines, and eventually to the terminal. I found an empty gate and took Gobi out to give her a drink. I heard some French people nearby count down and burst into cheers. I checked my watch. It was midnight. The most remarkable year of my life was over. The next adventure was about to begin.

"Listen, Gobi," I said to her. "You hear that? It means we bloody well did it! We made it here, and we're about to go. It's going to be a long journey, but trust me that it'll all be worth it. When we get to Edinburgh, you'll see; life is going to be amazing."

Air France made sure that the seat next to mine was empty, so even though Gobi had to stay in her carry-on bag for the duration, we travelled in style. She was a little unsettled as we took off, but as soon as I could put her bag on my lap, she calmed again.

I watched the in-flight map and waited until we flew over the Gobi Desert. It put a smile on my face to see Urumqi flash up and think about the way a city I'd never heard of a year earlier had become so significant to me now.

The cabin lights were dimmed, and my fellow passengers went to sleep. I turned the seat into a bed and quietly took Gobi out of the bag. She had started to get a little restless again, but as soon as she curled up in my arm, she fell into a deep, deep sleep.

I closed my eyes and remembered what it felt like to run on the long day. I could feel the heat all over again, the way the air was so hot it threatened to scorch my lungs. I saw Tommy struggling to stand and remembered the desperate search for shade. I also remembered that even though I was faint and queasy and worried that I might not make it out alive, I knew that if I did, I would do everything I could to make sure that Gobi and I spent the rest of our lives together.

I couldn't hold back the tears when I saw Lucja at Charles de Gaulle Airport. Gobi, on the other hand, couldn't hold back the fourteen hours of pee that her little bladder had stored up. I'd taken puppy pads with me and tried to get her to do her business on the plane, but she had refused. Only when she stood on the highly polished floor right in the middle of the concourse did she finally feel ready to let go.

I was sure that the rest of the journey home was going to be a simple affair, and we even made a detour into the city to show Gobi the Eiffel Tower and the Arc de Triomphe. After that we headed north to Belgium first, and then on to Amsterdam and the home of Lucja's uncle, aunt, and cousins.

Seeing their excitement at meeting Gobi for the first time reminded me of the way people had responded to Gobi's story in 2016. The year had been full of sad news, from celebrity deaths to terrorist attacks. Much of the world had been divided by politics, but I'd read many comments from people who felt Gobi was one of the few good news stories that restored their faith in human nature. In a year marked by grief and fear, Gobi's story was a beacon of light.

After a shower and a rest, Lucja, Gobi, and I said goodbye to the family and made our way to the ferry terminal that was just around the corner from the house. Lucja had spent weeks persuading the ferry company to bend the rule that forced dog owners to leave their pets in their cars or keep the dogs in the kennels provided on board. There was no way that was going to work for Gobi, and the company had finally agreed that we could take her with us in a cabin.

So I thought boarding would be easy and we were going to be fine. Nothing could go wrong, could it?

Well, yes, it could. And it did. Almost.

The moment we handed over Gobi's pet passport at the check-in desk, the air changed. The woman behind the counter was flicking manically back and forth across the pages, a look of total confusion on her face.

"Do you need some help?" said Lucja in Dutch. "What are you looking for?"

"I can't read it," she said. "It's all in Chinese. If I can't read it, I can't let you on."

She called her superior over, and the two of them riffled through the pages all over again.

"We can't read it," said the boss. "You can't come on board."

Lucja had spent weeks learning about all the various requirements for moving a dog across borders, and she knew the rules inside out. She carefully and calmly showed both of them which stamp related to which vaccination, but it was no use. They weren't changing their minds, and until they did, Gobi was stuck in Holland.

Then I remembered the stack of paperwork that Kiki had given me for when we reached UK border control. It was all the same information but in English. I handed it all over, watched them look through it all carefully, and listened to them finally make some encouraging noises.

Eventually, with just a few minutes to spare, we got a smile and a stamp in Gobi's pet passport. We were good to go.

The next morning, driving off the ferry, Lucja and I looked at each other nervously. Would we get stopped by UK border control? Would they find some flaw in the paperwork and send Gobi to London for an extra quarantine period? We approached the booth, held hands, and were surprisingly waved straight through. No checks. No hassle. No delay. Gobi was in the UK.

The drive north to Scotland was slow and easy, and as we passed low-slung hills and wide-open moors, I let my mind drift. I thought about the promise I had made to Gobi and the six months it took to make it happen. I thought back to all the people who donated money to help, the volunteers who spent day and night searching, and all the people worldwide who sent support messages and prayed for us. It wasn't just me who made this happen; it was the collective power of generous, loving people.

These thoughts brought a tear to my eye. The world was still a loving, kind place.

As the long journey home drew to a close, we drove over the hill and stared at the view. All of Edinburgh was laid out before us: Arthur's Seat—the mountain that stands guard over the city—the beach to the east, the Pentland Hills to the west. It was a beautiful day, not just because of the clear sky and clean air, and not even because it was my forty-second birthday.

It was perfect because of one simple, single reason.

We were together.

We made our way into the city, the car silent but our heads and hearts full. Turning onto our street, I realized I'd never thought about what it would feel like to walk through my front door, this remarkable little dog tucked under my arm.

I'd never thought about it because I'd never allowed myself to believe it would happen. All the deceit, all the fear, all the worry had weighed heavily on me. I'd never allowed myself the luxury of believing we'd finally do it.

But as the door opened and I saw good friends and loved ones inside, heard the popping of champagne corks and the cheers of people who were there to celebrate with us, I knew exactly what it felt like.

It felt like the beginning of a wonderful new adventure.

The hours and days that followed were busy in ways that reminded me of Urumqi. A TV crew had flown all the way from Australia to capture our return home and interview me. We received calls from journalists all over the world—some I knew well; others I had never spoken to before. They all wanted to know how Gobi had coped with the journey and what life held in store for her now.

I told them all how quickly she was adjusting to this new life, and how she and Lara the cat had already teamed up and taken joint ownership of the couch in our living room. I said that Gobi was an inspiration because she had dealt with the journey as she had dealt with every challenge thrown at her since we met. I told them I was proud of her.

But that was only part of the story. More than a handful of answers would be needed to say everything I wanted to say about Gobi. And sharing the ways in which finding Gobi had changed me would take even longer—especially as I was aware that this new life had only just begun.

Only Gobi knows the answer to many of the questions: Why was she wandering in the Tian Shan? Why did she pick me? What happened when she went missing?

What mattered most then and what still matters most today is this: from the moment I said yes to Gobi, my life has been different. Gobi has turned up the contrast. She has added to all the good things in my life and brought healing to some of the bad.

Gobi's hip has healed, and the hair has grown back where she had to be shaved for the operation. She doesn't squeal in pain if the site is inadvertently touched. When walking on soft ground, she will sometimes lift her leg slightly. The vet in Edinburgh says that's likely a memory habit because placing weight on that hip used to be painful. When Gobi and I now run the hills and trails, her stride is perfect, and keeping up with her is just as difficult as it was in the Gobi Desert.

That first night when we all were finally together, Gobi and Lara took up residence at the foot of the bed, and I heard again the familiar silence of home. Lucja turned to me and quietly asked what I wanted to do the next morning. We had nothing planned, and the first few hours of the day were ours.

I knew exactly what I wanted. I looked at Gobi and then back at Lucja.

"Let's all go for a run."

Acknowledgements

CHINA HAS BROUGHT SO MUCH GOOD TO MY life, and I am grateful to have spent so long a time there. In a country of more than one billion souls, I have met some of the most generous, thoughtful, and kind people I could ever hope to meet.

Kiki Chen was the one person who stuck with us from the start and made getting Gobi out of China actually happen. Chris Barden was a genuine "dog whisperer" who set up our search team and was instrumental in finding Gobi. To Lu Xin, I owe so much. She never stopped looking for Gobi and showed me what true generosity looks like. Jiuyen (Lil) was more than a translator, and her words helped me every day in the toughest of circumstances. I am profoundly grateful to all the volunteers who searched day and night for a dog they had never seen, to help a guy they had never met. I can never thank them enough but hope they know how important they are to this story.

To the Ma family, I owe great thanks for finding Gobi. WorldCare Pet's support and guidance was second to none, and the WorldCare Pet team in Beijing showed unconditional love, care, and dedication to Gobi around the clock.

I still smile when I think of the times I spent with the Urumqi boys from Lvbaihui Tribes Barbecue restaurant (especially when I remember the firewater they gave me. *Ganbei Maotai!*).

I miss my Beijing brothers from Ebisu Sushi and am proud to be able to call the city of Urumqi my home city in China. I do not know a more supportive, kind, and generous city on earth.

The Chinese media showed support and dedication for our story and the love within.

Back home in the UK, reuniting with Gobi could not have happened without Lisa Anderson, who looked after Lara and kept our house a home. Iona, Kris, Tony, and Gill are just a few of the wonderful people who supported Lucja throughout it all. And Ross Lawrie, I just have one thing to say to you: bobby-dazzler!

The media has played such an important part in this story. Jonathan Brown from the *Daily Mirror* was the first reporter to bring the story to press, Judy Tait brought the story to BBC Radio 5 Live, and host Phil Williams supported us from the start. They saw the story in ways that I did not, and they led the way in sharing it with others.

Invaluable support also has come from the BBC UK and World Services, Christian DuChateau at CNN, Amy Wang at the *Washington Post*, Deborah Hastings at *Inside Edition*, Oliver Thring at *The Times*, Victor Ferreira at the *Canadian Post*, Nick Farrow and Steve Pennels at Channel 7 Australia, Pip Tomson at ITV's *Good Morning Britain*, and the *Eric Zane Show* podcast.

To all the many other journalists and radio and television hosts who covered the story, I am thankful for your help in sharing our journey.

So many people have donated money, sent messages of love and support, or prayed every day for us. They didn't just believe in us—they made this whole thing possible.

I also want to thank Winston Chao; Mark Webber, for the tweet (Aussie Grit!); and Dr Chris Brown for his help, knowledge, and guidance. Richard Henson, who was an absolute legend, coming all the way to Urumqi to help. Tommy Chen, for being a great competitor and ambassador for Taiwan. Running coach Donnie Campbell, "one-two-three-one-two-three"; WAA Ultra Equipment, for standing by me; and William Grant and Sons, the kindest employers a man could wish for. Thanks are also due to DFDS Seaways and Air China.

Lastly, I am thankful for Team Dion and Gobi. Thanks to his daughter, Quinn, Paul de Souza made all of this a reality. Jay Kramer offered invaluable support, advice, and experience. Matt Baugher backed us and believed in us, and we owe him and all of the team at W Publishing, Thomas Nelson, and HarperCollins immense thanks for working so hard against such a tight deadline. Craig Borlase's vision, guidance, and patience putting this book together were incredible.

About the Author

DION LEONARD, a forty-two-year-old Australian, lives in Edinburgh, Scotland, with his wife, Lucja. Dion has not only completed but also competed for the top prize in some of the toughest ultra-marathons across the planet's most inhospitable landscapes: the brutal Moroccan Sahara Desert, twice in the 155-mile Marathon des Sables, and twice across South Africa's Kalahari Desert, also 155 miles.

During Dion's 155-mile race across the Gobi Desert in China, he fell in love with a stray dog (later named Gobi) who followed him during the week and changed both of their lives forever.